THE CONSTITUTION: FLOOR MISSING

A Revaluation of Founding Principles

RAVINDER NATH BHALLA MD

Contents

The Constitution: Floor Missing
A Revaluation of Founding Principles
Book Six of The Abundance Series

ISBN: 978-1-971562-40-7 ebook
978-1-971562-38-4 paperback
978-1-971562-39-1 hardback

First Edition, 2026
Printed in the United States of America

"I have not learned blindness yet.
That is my only credential."
— The Child

For every child still standing in the gap.

Preface

Five books is a long way to travel before arriving at the question you were always trying to answer.

The Abundance Series began where all honest clinical work begins: with the patient in front of you. Forty years of practice — mostly with children and families, mostly in communities that had very little — produced a framework before it produced a theory. Two orientations are available to human beings in any situation. The scarcity orientation reads the world as a place of threat, limitation, and zero-sum competition. The abundance orientation reads the same world as a place of possibility and expandable capacity. Neither is fixed at birth. Both are learned. And the orientation a person brings to their decisions shapes those decisions more than almost anything else.

The first book established that framework. The second examined how it operates inside the individual mind. The third applied it to artificial intelligence. The fourth addressed the people in power directly. The fifth went domain by domain through the policy landscape — healthcare, education, housing, criminal justice, the environment — and documented what the scarcity orientation builds and what the abundance orientation would build instead.

Five books. One persistent question: why does the abundance orientation keep losing, even when the evidence for it is overwhelming?

This book is the answer.

The answer is architectural. The scarcity orientation keeps winning because the documents that authorize the systems were written, at their founding, by people whose scarcity orientation won the close calls. What is encoded in a founding document does not change through ordinary policy. It shapes what policy is possible.

I came to this document from the outside. I immigrated to the United States in 1982. I did not grow up reading the Constitution as sacred text or the founders as mythological figures. I encountered it as an adult, with a clinical instrument rather than a political position — the child test, developed across forty years of practice. That instrument asks one question of every provision: what does this produce for the child with no buffer between herself and what the document actually delivers? Not what it promises. What it produces.

The child's voice runs through this book — in the poems, in the interstitials, in the Epilogue. It is not my critique. The founders themselves wrote the word posterity into the Preamble. The child is only asking what that word meant and whether the provisions delivered it. Her body does not accept rationalizations. It only receives or fails to receive what it needs. That is why the child test is the one measure the entire apparatus of constitutional argument cannot absorb.

I am nearly 68 years old. I will not live to see what this book's argument might eventually produce. That is not a reason to write it differently. It is the reason to write it honestly.

The Abundance Series named the systems. This book names the document that makes the systems necessary.

A word about how this book was written. No important book is written alone. The blind spots that any single perspective carries are exactly that — blind. You cannot see them from inside them. The friends who read early versions of these six volumes, who argued back, who named what I was missing, who said you are criticizing the document but not acknowledging what it has protected — these conversations are in every chapter. They are what the book means when it argues for the abundance orientation: you cannot build abundance alone. You reach further with others than without them.

This book also benefited from something that did not exist when I began the Abundance Series. AI served as research instrument, structural advisor, revision partner, and sounding board throughout the writing. What would have taken a year to research and draft was accomplished in weeks. I have worked with AI intensively over these past months and watched it improve with leaps and bounds — the tool I am using today is not the tool I began with. The trajectory is unmistakable, and the possibilities it opens for the kind of civic reasoning Chapter Eleven describes are only beginning to be visible. The friends broadened my perspective. The AI extended my reach. Both are expressions of the abundance orientation: you see further when you are willing to be helped.

Ravinder Nath Bhalla, MD
Ridgewood, New Jersey · March 2026

The Abundance Series: A Brief Account

The six books of the Abundance Series form a single sustained argument, approached from six different angles. Each book can be read independently. Together, they constitute a clinical examination of the scarcity orientation — what it is, how it operates, what it builds, and what it prevents — across the full range of human organization, from the individual mind to the founding document.

Book 1: *Abundance: Beyond Scarcity and Self-Devouring Cycles*

The foundational volume. Establishes the clinical framework distinguishing the scarcity orientation from the abundance orientation across individual, institutional, and civilizational scales. Draws on forty years of clinical practice to document how the scarcity orientation produces self-devouring cycles — systems that consume the conditions of their own continuation. Introduces the Nietzschean framework of revaluation as the mechanism by which the shift from scarcity to abundance thinking becomes possible. The snake-eating-its-tail metaphor originates here.

Book 2: *The Two Minds: Choosing Abundance over Scarcity*

The individual-psychological volume. Examines how the two orientations operate inside the human mind — as competing neural and behavioral patterns, not fixed personality types. Documents the conditions under which trauma, threat, and deprivation lock the scarcity orientation in place, and the conditions under which the abundance orientation becomes available as a choice. Includes clinical observations, philosophical analysis, and the poetry that has accompanied this work throughout.

Book 3: *Red Lines Rising: Governing AI While We Still Can*

The AI governance volume. Applies the abundance framework to artificial intelligence — the most consequential technological development in human history — and asks what governing it from the scarcity orientation would produce. Identifies the red lines that must not be crossed if AI is to serve the general welfare rather than concentrate power in the hands of those who already have it. Argues that the window for effective governance is open but closing.

Book 4: *The Abundance Dispatch: Letters to Power*

The operational companion volume. Addressed directly to the people with the most power to change the systems the series has documented: world leaders, corporate principals, engineers, and builders. Structured as open letters, it makes the case that the scarcity orientation is not only morally costly but strategically self-defeating — that the people who benefit most from the current arrangement are also the people who will lose most when it fails. Introduces the boardroom as the modern equivalent of the Philadelphia Convention.

Book 5: *Building Abundance: What We Ought to Create*

The policy volume. Proceeds domain by domain through the institutions that shape human life — healthcare, education, housing, criminal justice, election architecture, the environment, foreign aid, the distribution of AI's benefits — and documents what the scarcity orientation has built in each domain, what the abundance orientation would build instead, and what the child test reveals about the gap between them. The fifth book is where the series arrives at its policy conclusions. This sixth book asks why those conclusions keep losing, and names the foundation.

The Constitution: Floor Missing is the sixth volume. It is the book the series was pointing toward from the beginning — the explanation of why the policy argument keeps losing even when the evidence is overwhelming. The previous five books named the systems. This one names the document that makes the systems necessary.

A Note on Abundance Philosophy

The Abundance Series rests on a clinical observation made over forty years of practice, mostly with children and families in communities with very few resources: two orientations are available to any human being in any situation, and which one a person brings to their decisions shapes those decisions more than almost anything else. The first is the scarcity orientation — a reading of the world as a place of threat, limitation, and zero-sum competition, in which someone else's gain is your loss, in which protection and hoarding are rational responses to an environment that is fundamentally hostile. The second is the abundance orientation — a reading of the same world as a place of possibility and expandable capacity, in which the conditions of human flourishing are not fixed and finite but can be grown, shared, and compounded.

These are not moral categories. They are clinical ones. The scarcity orientation is not evil — it is the adaptive response of a nervous system that has been shaped by real threat, real deprivation, real experience of what happens when resources are withdrawn. The abundance orientation is not naive — it is the orientation of the child before the scarcity lessons are learned, and it is recoverable in the adult through the right conditions, the right relationships, and the right understanding of what the scarcity orientation costs. The core clinical finding, documented across forty years of practice and five previous volumes, is this: the scarcity orientation self-devours. Systems organized around it consume the conditions of their own continuation — they extract until there is nothing left, exclude until the excluded become the threat, protect the defended position until the defended position becomes the source of the harm. The abundance orientation compounds. Systems organized around it produce more than they consume, include rather than exclude, and build the conditions under which more is possible for more people over time.

The Nietzschean concept of revaluation — returning to the founding values of any system and asking what they are for, who they serve, and whether the machinery built to honor them is delivering what was announced — is the philosophical method throughout the series. Friedrich Nietzsche argued that the values a culture operates by are not eternal truths but historical formations, encoding the interests and orientations of the people who established them. To revaluate is not to destroy — it is to see clearly, without the mythological scaffolding that makes the established order appear natural and inevitable, and to ask honestly whether what was built is delivering what was promised. That is the question this series has been asking across six books: what was promised, what was built, and what the gap between them costs the person with no buffer between herself and what the system actually delivers. The child. Always the child. She is the measure because she is the one who cannot compensate for what the system withholds. Her body holds the answer before any philosophy has been written.

A Note on the Founding Moment

A note on what this book's title diagnoses. A floor is what stands between the person at the bottom and the fall. In a building, a missing floor is not a design preference or an oversight — it is a structural deficiency, a condition that must be named before it can be addressed. The Constitution: Floor Missing is this book's clinical finding applied to the foundational document of American life. The Constitution contains walls and ceilings in abundance — protections against what the government may do to you, limits on the concentration of power, enumerated rights that have been litigated and extended across two and a half centuries. What it does not contain is a floor: an affirmative obligation to provide the conditions of human development to the child who has no buffer between herself and what the document actually delivers. That absence is the diagnosis. The title is the finding.

The word that makes the absence most visible is one the founders placed in the Preamble themselves: posterity. Those who come after us. The children, the grandchildren, the generations who will inherit whatever is built without being consulted about the building. The founders announced that the document was not only for the people in the room — it was for posterity. This book holds the document to that announcement. It asks whether what was built delivers what was promised to the people who had no voice in the building — starting with the child.

The United States was founded twice — once in words, once in law.

The first founding was the Declaration of Independence, adopted in 1776. The men who signed it knew the stakes. Benjamin Harrison joked to the thinner Elbridge Gerry that Harrison would die quickly when they were hanged for treason while Gerry would dangle longer. They were signing what might be their death warrants.

The Declaration's central sentence — all men are created equal, endowed with certain unalienable rights — stated the abundance vision at its fullest. But the document that emerged was already a compromised version of what had been proposed. An entire passage condemning the slave trade as a cruel war against human nature was removed before adoption. Southern colonies would not sign a document that condemned the institution their economies depended on. Northern merchants who profited from the trade would not either. The abundance vision was present at the first founding. So was the mechanism of its removal.

Eleven years later, in the summer of 1787, fifty-five delegates gathered in Philadelphia to replace the failing Articles of Confederation with something that could actually govern. They were not the idealists of 1776. They were practical men, exhausted by years of near-collapse, trying to construct something durable. And many of them were genuinely, deeply conflicted about what they were doing.

Benjamin Franklin was the oldest at eighty-one, the most internationally respected, and in many ways the most honest about the dangers ahead. He had spent decades in Europe watching how concentrated power corrupted institutions. He proposed that the executive receive no salary — arguing that combining power and profit in one position would attract precisely the wrong people. He was voted down. He proposed opening each session with prayer when the debates grew dangerous. The proposal was not adopted — practical objections were raised, including the absence of funds for a chaplain, and the convention had already proceeded weeks without one. When he left the convention and a woman asked what they had produced, he said: a republic, if you can keep it. That is not optimism. It is a warning from a man who understood what concentrated power does to republics over time.

James Madison arrived having studied every confederacy in recorded history. He was thirty-six, the most intellectually prepared man in the room, carrying a vision of national government broad enough to provide for the general welfare of every person who lived under it. He would watch most of that vision be negotiated away over four months — and then spend the rest of his life managing what that loss had made of him.

Alexander Hamilton feared what he called the turbulence of democracy — the capacity of ordinary people to be misled into destroying the republic. Elbridge Gerry, who had joked with Harrison about hanging, refused to sign the final document because he believed it gave too much power to too few. George Mason demanded a bill of rights and did not get one. He refused to sign as well.

These men feared concentrated power. They had just fought a war against it. And yet the document they produced concentrated power in their own hands and the hands of people like them, while constructing elaborate protections against everyone else's power. They could see the corrupting influence of power when it threatened to flow toward others. They could not see it when it flowed toward themselves.

Madison's Federalist No. 10 makes this visible. He argues brilliantly that factions — interest groups pursuing their own benefit at others' expense — will always try to capture government, and that a large republic with competing factions is the best protection against any one faction dominating. What he does not name is that the convention itself was a faction: propertied, educated, commercially connected, overwhelmingly slaveholding. The document they produced protected that faction's interests more reliably than anyone else's. He diagnosed the disease in others and prescribed a cure that left his own group untreated.

On the convention's final day, Franklin looked at the carved sun on the back of Washington's chair and said he had wondered throughout the proceedings whether it was rising or setting. He had concluded it was rising. He was right that something new had begun. Whether it was rising for everyone is the question this book examines.

One pattern connects both foundings. The clause condemning the slave trade was removed from the Declaration not because delegates disagreed with it but because agreement on it would have broken the coalition. The vision was present. It was set aside when the defended positions of the people in the room required it. The Constitutional Convention repeated that pattern eleven years later, close call after close call.

The Federalist Papers and the Anti-Federalist responses that eventually won a Bill of Rights are the public record of what the founders understood the document to mean and what they feared it might become. Both sides were right about something. What neither side debated was the question this book examines: not what the government could do to citizens, but what it was obligated to do for them. That question was not asked. And neither side asked a related question: who counts as a citizen? Women could not vote — suffrage, the legal right to cast a ballot and choose representatives, was denied to women until 1920. Children were not contemplated at all. The we the people who ordained and established the Constitution were a small fraction of the actual people living under it. Its absence is where the reading begins.

Prologue: The Trauma Document

Before examining what the Constitution contains, examine what produced it. The document was written by men who had survived a revolution — not observed one, survived one. They had watched colleagues die, financed a war on borrowed credit, and lived for eight years with the possibility that everything they were building would be destroyed. When it was over, they carried what survivors carry: a nervous system reorganized around threat, a deep conviction that the world is a place of scarcity — of safety, of trust, of time. This is not a criticism. It is a diagnosis.

Trauma narrows vision. It makes protection feel more urgent than possibility. It elevates what can be defended — land, property, sovereignty — over what might be built. When traumatized people negotiate under pressure, in a group, the scarcity orientation does not average out. It compounds. Each person's defended position becomes the minimum the next person will accept. The room produces the arithmetic of fear, not the wisdom of its members. The Philadelphia Convention of 1787 was that room.

The Preamble — written last, by one gifted writer, after the provisions were already settled — carries the abundance vision: general welfare, the blessings of liberty, posterity. It is the part of the document that knows what health looks like. The provisions are the defended self — the part that could not, in that room, under that pressure, trust the vision enough to make it law.

The child test asks one question of every provision: what does this produce for the child with no buffer between herself and what the document actually delivers? Not what it promises. What it produces. The Preamble mentions posterity. The provisions do not protect it. That gap is not an oversight. It is what happens when the scarcity orientation wins the close calls.

Trauma is not resolved by writing it into law. It is transmitted. The constitutional architecture has functioned for two and a half centuries as an inherited nervous system — passing forward not the founders' wisdom but their defenses, encoded in provisions made deliberately resistant to change. The amendment process requiring three-quarters of states is not democratic caution. It is the document's immune system, protecting itself from the reexamination that healing would require.

What is written in fear, and made unchangeable, does not become wisdom with age. It becomes the definition of normal.

The three provisions that follow are where the scarcity orientation won the most consequential close calls. Each had an abundance alternative. Each alternative was present and argued. Each time, the defended position prevailed.

The Child Speaks

I would bow to you, Great Ones,
but I have not yet learned how.
No one has taught me to make myself small
in the presence of power.
Forgive me — or do not.
I do not yet know that I need your forgiveness.

I am the human child.
I arrived before your arguments,
before your compromises,
before the room closed its windows
and began its long negotiation
with fear.

My body knows what you have forgotten.
Nietzsche said it plainly:
your body holds more wisdom
than all the philosophy in the world.
I am that wisdom,
still undefeated,

still undefended,
still making its original claim
without apology.

I am abundance incarnate.
I am born of infinite possibilities
and infinite impossibilities —
both, together, in this small body
that needs to be fed,
held,
kept warm,
kept safe.
Not as a favor.
As a fact.

I am what you were
before the war taught you to defend.
I am what your grandchildren will be
when they arrive
into whatever you have built
or failed to build.

I am the reminder
you encoded out of your document.
You wrote posterity in the first sentence
and then constructed a machinery
with no obligation to deliver it.

I am posterity.
I am standing here.

You would have died for liberty —
and many of you did.
You recognized justice
the moment it was denied to you —
and felt its absence in your bones.

But when you finally held both in your hands,
you did not know how to open them
for anyone outside the room.
Not from cruelty.
From a scarcity so deep
you could not see it.
Liberty felt finite.
Justice felt exhaustible.
If others received them fully,
something would be taken
from what you had bled to keep.

My body has not learned that arithmetic.
I do not yet know that liberty runs out.
I do not yet know that justice
must be rationed,
born out of fear and anxiety.

Rise —
not for my sake.
I will survive or I will not,
and the document will not be the reason
either way.

Rise for your own sake.
For the body's sake.
For the wisdom your negotiation traded away
in a closed room in summer heat
when you were doing the best you could
and it was not enough.

Your free will is still yours.
Liberty — the thing you crossed oceans for,
the thing you bled for —
is still available.
Justice — the thing you yearned for

and grasped and then withheld —
is still possible.

Use them now
for the ones who cannot yet
make themselves small enough
to fit inside your room.

I have not learned blindness yet.
That is my only credential.
It is enough.

-RNB

PART I

THE DIAGNOSIS

The American Constitution as Clinical Artifact

1

The Room

Philadelphia, May 1787. The city is the largest in the new nation — which is not yet functioning as one. The Articles of Confederation have produced eight years of near-collapse: war debts unpaid, currencies worthless, states taxing each other like foreign countries, a continental army that dissolved itself because no one could fund it. Fifty-five delegates will eventually attend, though numbers fluctuate as men arrive late, leave early, or walk out when proceedings move in directions they cannot accept. The windows are closed — against the summer heat and against the possibility that what is being said inside might reach the public too soon. The secrecy rule is agreed unanimously on the second day. What happens in this closed room, among men who have survived the same unsurvivable thing, under pressure, in summer heat — this is what the chapter examines. Not as political history alone. As clinical event.

BEFORE THE CLINICAL READING BEGINS, one obstacle must be named.

The founders are revered. Not merely respected — revered.

They have been made into mythological figures whose wisdom is assumed and whose document is treated as sacred text. In schools, in civic rituals, in the physical architecture of Washington, in the way the Constitution itself is displayed under glass — the reverence is structural. It serves a function.

That function is this: the founders' greatness justifies the document's authority. To question the design feels like an attack on the legitimacy of everything built on it. This is why constitutional critique consistently produces personal affront — not because the argument is wrong, but because the mythology has been absorbed so completely that questioning it feels like a violation of something sacred.

This book does not attack the founders. It reads their chart. A patient's accomplishments do not exempt their pathology from examination. The founders' accomplishments do not exempt their document from the child test.

One voice cannot be silenced by reverence or argued away by legal sophistication. The child's voice. The child who inherits what the document provides and what it withholds. Who cannot compensate for its absences with political standing or education. The child test is not the author's critique. It is the founders' own criterion — they wrote posterity into the Preamble — returned to ask whether the provisions delivered it.

With that established, enter the room.

BEGIN with who is in the room.

The delegates are extraordinary men. Lawyers, planters, merchants, soldiers, political theorists. Their median age is forty-two — young enough to have fought the revolution, old enough to have watched it nearly destroy what it built. Eight signed the Declaration of Independence. Washington, who presides without speaking much, is the most famous man in the Western world — the general who won the war and then gave up power, an act the world found almost incomprehensible.

They are also, without exception, men of property. Many are wealthy. A significant number — including Madison and Washington — are slaveholders. They carry into the room not only their political theories but their ledgers.

The trauma of the revolution was not evenly distributed. A Massachusetts merchant's experience was not a Virginia planter's experience, though both survived the same war. The fears in the room are not identical. What these men share is the nervous system reorganization of people who have passed through prolonged existential threat. What they do not share is what specifically threatens them now.

No one in the room has fully processed what they have been through. The revolution ended four years ago. In the intervening years, they moved directly from unsurvivable experience into managing its aftermath. The processing was deferred. The defenses remained. Now they are in a closed room in summer heat, negotiating the architecture of a new government, carrying those defenses with them.

This is not a criticism of their intelligence. Many are among the most sophisticated political thinkers of their century. It is an observation about what happens to even sophisticated intelligence when the nervous system has been reorganized by prolonged threat. The mind can hold the abundance vision — can articulate it with extraordinary clarity — while the body votes for the defended position when the close call arrives.

The trauma argument runs deeper than the founders' nervous systems. It runs to the bottom of what human beings are. Feelings are the foundation of every human decision — not the surface feelings that words can name, but the layered architecture that developmental science has spent a century beginning to map. The deepest layer forms earliest: in infancy, during the attachment phase, when the infant's nervous system is calibrated against the emotional world of its caregivers. That calibration is colored by inherited temperament — the biological substrate that arrives before any experience — and by the complex emotional inheritance of the people who hold and feed and speak to the child in those first years. The bottom layer is not rigid. It is dynamic, interlaying with every subsequent experience. But it is the most fixed and the most determinative. Every feeling that comes later — every fear, every love, every political conviction, every constitutional close call — sits on top of it.

Feelings are also profoundly contagious. One person's fear activates another's. Groups amplify this effect dramatically. A crowd does not produce the average of its members' emotional states. It produces something more intense — polarized, simplified, driven toward the most activated feeling in the room. A crowd of frightened men is not fifty-five frightened men. It is a single frightened organism with fifty-five bodies. The Philadelphia Convention was exactly this: men isolated in a sealed room through a Philadelphia summer, under deadline, with the union threatening to collapse at every close call. Their bottom-layer fears — formed in infancy, shaped by revolution, activated by urgency — were being amplified by the group. The rational deliberation the history books describe was real. And it was sitting on top of a foundation of contagious fear that no one in the room could fully see, because you cannot see your own bottom layer from inside it. That is the nature of the bottom layer. It operates beneath visibility. This is what the child test bypasses. The child has not yet developed the upper layers that cover the bottom. She has not learned the rationalizations, the ideological scaffolding, the legal reasoning that makes the bottom layer invisible. She operates from the bottom layer directly. That is not her weakness. It is her credential.

There is a deeper structural problem with the moment itself. The most consequential long-term commitments tend to be made at the moment of maximum urgency — when immediate need clouds the judgment that long-term thinking requires. The philosopher Friedrich Nietzsche observed this about marriage: that the most important and pivotal decision in a person's life is typically made at the moment of least capacity for the long-term judgment it demands, and he proposed a provisional small marriage before the permanent one as a remedy. The observation applies with clinical precision to the Philadelphia Convention. The founders were not making a considered long-term choice about the constitutional architecture best suited to their posterity. They were making the minimum viable agreement necessary to prevent immediate dissolution — under emergency conditions, in four months, with the union threatening to collapse at every close call. The document that emerged reflected those conditions as much as it reflected any deliberate vision. Several later constitutional moments understood this instinctively. South Africa used an interim constitution to govern its transition from apartheid while the substantive document was developed through two years of deliberate public process. India's constituent assembly deliberated for nearly three years before adopting its final text. The American founders had no such interval. The emergency produced the document. The immune system then ensured that the deliberation the emergency foreclosed could not easily occur afterward.

THE CHILD TEST BELONGS HERE, before the provisions, because it is the instrument that makes the clinical reading possible. For any provision, any clause, ask: what does this produce for the child with no buffer between herself and what it actually delivers? Not what it promises. Not what its authors intended. What it produces. A founding document is addressed to the future — the Preamble announces this directly: the blessings of liberty secured to ourselves and our posterity. Posterity means children, the people who will inherit whatever is built in this room without being consulted about the building. The child has the diagnostic property of having no resources to compensate. An adult with property, education, and political standing can navigate a constitutional architecture that provides no affirmative floor. The child born without those buffers cannot. She receives what the document actually delivers. She is the most accurate measure of its real design. The child test is not sentimental. It is precise. It asks the hardest version of the question: what does this produce for the person who cannot compensate for what it fails to provide?

THE CONVENTION OPENS MAY 25, 1787. Washington is elected president by unanimous vote. The secrecy rule is adopted. Then the Virginia delegation presents Madison's plan — a genuinely national government acting directly on individuals, not through states, with broad authority over matters of general welfare. It is the most ambitious vision in the room. It is also, politically, a large-state document. Proportional representation in both chambers would give Virginia, Pennsylvania, and Massachusetts dominant power, and the small states see this immediately. Their scarcity orientation — the fear of being swallowed, of losing what they have — activates from the opening day. What follows is six weeks of foundational negotiation. The abundance vision functions as aspiration. The scarcity orientation functions as floor. The final document will be whatever the aspiration can achieve above the defended positions of the men who will not go lower.

The Great Compromise — proportional representation in the House, equal representation in the Senate — is the structural resolution. Not a triumph of wisdom. The minimum viable agreement among men whose trust in each other is limited by the arithmetic of their interests. The Senate encodes the scarcity logic of the small states permanently into the legislative architecture. The child test applied to this chamber finds one where the weight of a citizen's political voice depends on which state she was born in — where Wyoming and California are constitutionally equivalent, and where rural, less populous states will persistently outweigh the places where most people live.

BY MID-JULY the legislature is settled. The room turns to harder questions — and beneath all of them, deferred but unavoidable, the question of slavery.

The slavery debates show the scarcity orientation at its most unmediated. The three-fifths number was not derived from any principle. It is what the negotiation produced. Northern states did not want enslaved people counted for representation because counting them would inflate Southern power without giving those people any of the rights that representation is meant to protect. Southern states wanted full counting because it meant power. Three-fifths was what each side needed to stay at the table.

What is clinically significant is what happens to the men in the room during this debate. Delegates capable of extraordinary moral clarity in other contexts become suddenly procedural, suddenly practical. The trauma-informed defense mechanism is familiar: when a moral confrontation threatens the defended position too directly, the defended mind moves to process. It stops asking is this right and starts asking can we make this work.

Madison knows slavery is dehumanizing — he acknowledges as much in his private correspondence. He owns over one hundred enslaved people at Montpelier. He writes the Virginia Plan with its broad national authority that could, in principle, address slavery. He then negotiates the three-fifths compromise, the protection of the slave trade until 1808, and signs the document that encodes both. The abundance vision and the defended position, in the same man, at the same table, producing the same document.

This is not hypocrisy in the simple sense. It is what unprocessed trauma and unchallenged property interest produce together, in a room under pressure. The vision survives as rhetoric. The defense survives as law.

There is a deeper layer. These men had not merely survived a monarchy. They had been formed inside one — shaped by a system where power was concentrated, property was protected for those who held it, and the people at the bottom existed to generate wealth for those at the top. They fought that system. They defeated it. And then, in Philadelphia, they reproduced its structure.

The clinical term is identification with the aggressor. It describes what happens when people who have survived domination unconsciously adopt the dominator's logic — not from admiration, but from the psychic necessity of having survived it. You cannot defeat what you cannot, at some level, become. Having become it to survive, you cannot easily un-become it when the threat is gone.

The founders did not replace the monarchy. They distributed it. Each delegate became the monarch of his state's interest, his property's protection, his faction's survival. The people they governed — the enslaved, the propertyless, the women, the children the Preamble invoked as posterity — inherited the role that all of them had occupied under the British crown: the subject whose existence the system required and whose welfare it was not designed to protect.

This is what makes the reverence clinically interesting. A population identifies with its founders not merely out of admiration but out of a shared sense of liberation. To question the founders is, psychologically, to question the liberation itself. The defended position protects itself by making critique feel like an attack on freedom.

The child test bypasses this entirely. The child did not participate in the liberation. She arrived afterward, into whatever the liberation built. She is not invested in the mythology. She has only her body and its needs and the question of whether the document provides for them.

~

BY EARLY SEPTEMBER the provisions are substantially settled. The convention appoints a Committee of Style. Gouverneur Morris, the primary writer, drafts the Preamble.

Note the sequence. The Preamble is written after the provisions. The mission statement is composed after the machinery is built. We the People of the United States, in Order to form a more perfect Union, establish Justice, insure domestic Tranquility, provide for the common defence, promote the general Welfare, and secure the Blessings of Liberty to ourselves and our Posterity — drafted in the final days, as a rhetorical frame for a document whose decisions have already been made.

The Preamble is sincere. Morris means it. The delegates who read it mean it. But it is applied to provisions negotiated by defended positions of traumatized men protecting their states, their property, and their survival.

The result is a document with a split structure. The Preamble is the self that knows what health looks like. The provisions are the defended self — the self that could not, in that room, trust the vision enough to operationalize it.

The child test applied to the Preamble: it promises her posterity. It announces that the document is addressed, in part, to her.

The child test applied to the provisions: they create no floor beneath her. No right to food, shelter, healthcare, or the conditions her development requires. The state cannot harm her directly. It has no obligation to sustain her.

The Preamble mentions posterity. The provisions do not protect it. That gap is not a failure of aspiration. It is what the defended positions produced when the close calls arrived.

ON SEPTEMBER 17, 1787, thirty-nine of the forty-two delegates then present sign the Constitution. Three refuse. Edmund Randolph, who proposed the Virginia Plan but cannot accept what it became. George Mason, who demanded a bill of rights and did not get one. Elbridge Gerry, whose objections are various and fundamental.

Benjamin Franklin, helped to the signing table, has prepared a speech read on his behalf. He cannot help but express a wish that every member with objections would doubt a little of their own infallibility and put their name to the document. He does not say it is sound. He says it is the best that could be obtained.

That is the clinical verdict. The Constitution is the best agreement that could be reached by those men, in that room, in that summer, carrying what they carried. It reflects the full tension of their moment — the genuine abundance aspiration and the genuine scarcity defense, both present, both real, both encoded.

It is not a roadmap for posterity. It is a peace treaty among the people in the room. Peace treaties encode who had leverage when the fighting stopped. They pass that leverage forward — not as wisdom but as structure — to people who were not present and were not consulted.

The child at the bottom — the child the Preamble invokes — inherits the peace treaty. She did not negotiate it. She cannot easily change it. She will spend her life navigating institutions shaped by the defended positions of men doing the best they could with what they had, in Philadelphia, in 1787.

The three provisions that follow are where the defended positions most consequentially won the close calls. Each had an abundance alternative. Each alternative was argued. Each time, the scarcity orientation prevailed.

The child test will be applied to each. The record is clear.

2

The Absent Floor

Begin with what Madison actually proposed. Before the compromises, before the provisions, before the negotiation began — there was a vision. Madison arrived in Philadelphia having spent months studying every confederacy in history, looking for the design failure that brought them all down. He found it consistently: a central government that acted on states rather than on individuals could not govern. It could pass resolutions. It could not enforce them. The Virginia Plan he drafted proposed a national government with authority to legislate in all cases to which the separate states were incompetent — broad, unencumbered by enumeration, acting directly on people rather than on governments. Read through the child test, it is the abundance orientation at its most expansive: a government with the power and the mandate to provide for the people who live under it. That government was in the room on May 29, 1787. Then the negotiation began.

~

THE NARROWING of Madison's vision happened in stages, and each stage has a clinical character worth examining.

The first stage was structural. The small states' resistance to proportional representation produced the Great Compromise — equal Senate representation regardless of population. This was not merely a political adjustment. It was the first encoding of the scarcity orientation into the document's machinery: the principle that state sovereignty, not human need, would be the organizing unit of the upper chamber. A government designed around state sovereignty rather than individual welfare will always privilege the protection of existing arrangements over the provision of new floors. The Senate, as designed, was a chamber built to prevent rather than to provide.

The second stage was more subtle and more consequential. As the convention progressed and the provisions took shape, the language of the general welfare survived — but its operational meaning was progressively emptied. The Taxing and Spending Clause gave Congress power to provide for the common Defence and general Welfare of the United States. This sounded like Madison's broad mandate. It was not. The clause authorized spending in service of general welfare. It did not obligate it. The state could choose to provide. It was not required to.

This distinction — between authorization and obligation, between permission and duty — is the constitutional deficit at the heart of this chapter. The difference it makes to the child at the bottom is total. Authorization means the state may feed her if it chooses, may house her if it chooses, may provide the conditions of her development if the political winds are favorable and the legislative calendar permits. Obligation means the state must — that she has a claim, that the claim is enforceable, that no political calculation can extinguish it.

The American Constitution chose authorization. It encoded no obligation. Each defended position in that room was reasonable in its own logic. The cumulative effect on the child the Preamble invoked was disastrous.

MADISON UNDERSTOOD what he had lost. His letters after the convention — particularly his correspondence with Jefferson in Paris — carry the tone of a man who knows the document is insufficient to the vision that produced it. He had wanted a national government that could act. He had gotten a national government that could, carefully, under specified conditions, with enumerated authority, when the states permitted, act. The difference between those two governments is the history of American social policy for the next two and a half centuries.

And then Madison did something that the clinical framework predicts and that the historical record confirms: under the pressure of the ratification debates, defending the document he had helped produce against Anti-Federalist attack, he completed the narrowing himself. In Federalist 41, published in January 1788, Madison argued that the general welfare language in the Taxing and Spending Clause was not a broad grant of power but a summary heading for the specific enumerated powers that followed it. The expansive phrase meant only what the list permitted. The abundance language was rhetorical. The scarcity interpretation was operational.

This argument was not forced on Madison from outside. It was made by the man who had conceived the abundance vision in the first place. The room had not merely prevented him from building what he envisioned. It had recruited him into the work of explaining why it could not be built.

The defended position had won. Not just in the document. Inside the document's author.

What was lost in that winning was not abstract. It was the floor. The constitutional obligation that would have meant, in practical terms, that the state had a duty to feed the child, house the child, provide the child with the conditions of her development. That obligation was within reach in May 1787. It was negotiated away by September. And it was then ratified, argued for, and defended by the man who had originally conceived it.

The abundance vision survived only as rhetoric — in a

Preamble written after the provisions were settled, by a man who was not Madison.

~

TWO CENTURIES LATER, the Supreme Court of the United States produced the clearest statement of what the absent floor actually means in a child's life. The case is DeShaney v. Winnebago County, decided in 1989. It is worth knowing in full.

Joshua DeShaney was born in 1979 in Wyoming. His parents divorced when he was a year old, and his father, Randy DeShaney, was awarded custody and moved to Winnebago County, Wisconsin. When Joshua was four, the county Department of Social Services began receiving reports that his father was beating him. What followed was a clinical record of institutional observation without obligation. A caseworker visited the home and noted suspicious injuries. The Department took no action. Joshua was hospitalized with injuries consistent with child abuse. The Department formed a monitoring team. The team recorded additional injuries over the following months — a cut forehead, bruises on the face, a scraped chin. The caseworker wrote in her file that she just knew the phone would ring someday and Joshua would be dead. She did nothing more, because the law required nothing more. She observed. She recorded. She predicted. She was correct. In March 1984, Randy DeShaney beat his four-year-old son so severely that Joshua suffered massive brain damage and fell into a coma. He survived, but was expected to spend the rest of his life in an institution for the profoundly mentally disabled. His father was convicted of child abuse and sentenced to two to four years in prison. He served less than two.

Joshua's mother, Melody DeShaney, sued Winnebago County on Joshua's behalf. She argued that the Department of Social Services had violated Joshua's constitutional rights by failing to protect him from violence that the Department had documented, monitored, and predicted. The case reached the Supreme Court, which ruled against Joshua seven to two.

Chief Justice William Rehnquist — appointed to the Court by President Nixon in 1972 and one of its most consistent voices for limiting federal constitutional reach — wrote the majority opinion. The Fourteenth Amendment's Due Process Clause, he held, is a limitation on what the state may do to a person. It is not a guarantee of protection from private harm. The Constitution confers no affirmative right to governmental aid, even where that aid might be necessary to secure a person's life or liberty. The state had not created the danger Joshua faced. His father had. The state therefore had no constitutional duty to protect Joshua from it.

Justice William Brennan dissented, joined by Justice Thurgood Marshall. Brennan had served on the Supreme Court since 1956 — appointed by President Eisenhower and serving for thirty-four years as the court's most influential voice for expanding constitutional protections to those most vulnerable to government indifference. In DeShaney, his dissent was not only a legal argument. It was a moral one. The state, he wrote, had inserted itself into Joshua's situation — opened a file, formed a monitoring team, displaced other potential sources of intervention. By doing so, it had made Joshua more dependent on state protection and more vulnerable when that protection failed to materialize. That, Brennan argued, constituted state action. The Constitution should have something to say about a government that watches a child being beaten, records what it sees, predicts his death, and does nothing.

The majority said no. The document protects against what the government does to you. It has no provision for what the government fails to do for you when you are four years old and your father is beating you in a county whose caseworkers have already written in their files that you are going to die. Apply the child test: it produces Joshua DeShaney. The caseworker's prediction, fulfilled. The majority opinion's precision — not cruelty, but the logical endpoint of a design choice made in Philadelphia in 1787. Brennan saw the child. Rehnquist saw the document. Both were reading the same words. Only one of them was wrong about what those words required.

Sixteen years later, the Supreme Court extended that logic to its most catastrophic conclusion. In Town of Castle Rock v. Gonzales (2005), Jessica Gonzales held a restraining order against her estranged husband. He violated it, took their three daughters from the front yard, and killed all three of them. The police had repeatedly refused to enforce the order when she called. The Supreme Court held seven to two that she had no constitutional claim. A restraining order — even one stating the police shall arrest the violator — does not create a constitutionally enforceable entitlement to police protection. Three children were dead. The document required nothing. DeShaney had said the state need not protect a child from private harm. Castle Rock said the state need not enforce its own legal instruments to protect children from death. The absent floor is not a historical artifact. It is the operating condition of American constitutional law today.

BEFORE TURNING to that global scale, one contemporary case bridges DeShaney directly to the present. In 2003, the mummified body of seven-year-old Faheem Williams was found in a basement storage bin in New Jersey. The state child welfare agency had failed to investigate multiple maltreatment reports. His brothers had been starved and abused by the same adoptive parents. The case produced public outrage, a settlement, and a court-ordered overhaul. A class action lawsuit filed in 1999 on behalf of more than six thousand children in state custody had already documented the same pattern: overburdened caseworkers, unsafe placements, children with serious psychiatric needs moved through a system unequipped to address them.

From this period of scandal and court oversight emerged PerformCare — a well-funded managed care organization that became the single point of access for New Jersey's most seriously troubled children, including those with severe psychiatric illness, developmental disabilities, and behavioral health crises. PerformCare had money, infrastructure, and reach. What it did not have — and what its design did not meaningfully incorporate — was psychiatric expertise at the level the children it served required. The system was built primarily by administrators. Clinical criteria were established by managed care logic. Psychiatrists were consulted minimally and largely ceremonially. The children flowing through PerformCare were among the most psychiatrically complex in the state. The expertise most essential to their care was the expertise least represented in the system designed to provide it. This is the absent floor reproduced at full scale, with full funding, by people who genuinely believed they were solving the problem — because without an affirmative obligation to provide what children actually need, even well-resourced systems will be built around what administrators can manage rather than what children require.

One more present-day expression of the absent floor must be named before turning to its global scale. Children held in United States immigration detention facilities have, in recent years, been documented living in overcrowded conditions without adequate medical care, without educational provision, and without the basic sanitation that human development requires. Some have died in custody from treatable conditions. These children are in a legally distinct position from Joshua DeShaney in one important respect: the state did not merely fail to intervene while a private actor caused harm. The state is the direct cause of their condition. It took them — in some cases from their parents — transported them, and placed them in the facilities where they are held. Under the DeShaney framework, this should create precisely the constitutional duty the majority denied Joshua: when the state creates the danger, it incurs the obligation to protect from it. That even this more direct state responsibility has been inconsistently enforced reveals the DeShaney architecture operating at its most nakedly extractive. The immigrant child — documented or undocumented, infant or adolescent — has been defined out of the posterity the Preamble announced. She is present in the country. She is counted when the counting serves institutional purposes. She is uncounted for the protections the document was meant to provide. The three-fifths template, updated.

Two hundred years before Joshua DeShaney, a different child

was being produced by the same logic — not in a Wisconsin county but on an island in the Caribbean, in a laboratory of what happens when the absent floor operates at civilizational scale.

Saint-Domingue — the French colony that would become Haiti — was in 1789 the most profitable colony in the Western world. It produced roughly forty percent of Europe's sugar and more than half its coffee, on the labor of approximately five hundred thousand enslaved Africans. The wealth it generated flowed to France, to the French crown, to the plantation owners, to the trading houses of Bordeaux and Nantes. The people who produced that wealth received nothing — no floor, no protection, no claim on the document that governed the society in which they lived. They were, in the constitutional arithmetic of their moment, not persons. They were property generating representation for the people who owned them.

In 1791, they revolted. The Haitian Revolution — the only successful slave revolution in human history — produced by 1804 the independent Republic of Haiti, the first Black republic in the Western hemisphere, governed by people who had been enslaved and who had liberated themselves by force.

The founders of the United States watched this revolution with the specific terror of people who recognized their own situation reflected in it. They had enslaved approximately seven hundred thousand people on their own soil. The Haitian Revolution demonstrated, with the precision of a clinical experiment, what happened when the absent floor was not merely a constitutional design choice but a lived condition pushed beyond what human beings could sustain. The people at the bottom, given the choice between the floor they had been denied and the violence required to claim it, chose the violence.

The American response was not to examine the floor. It was to quarantine the example. The United States refused to recognize Haiti diplomatically for fifty-eight years — until 1862, when the enslaved population of the American South was itself approaching revolt. American ports were closed to Haitian ships. The Haitian Revolution was suppressed in public discourse with the specific urgency of people who understood exactly what it meant.

The founders' anxiety about Haiti was not irrational. It was the scarcity orientation reading the evidence correctly and drawing the scarcity conclusion: if the floor remains absent, the people at the bottom will eventually take by force what the document refused to provide. The response to that anxiety was not to provide the floor. It was to reinforce the walls.

In 1825, France — under pressure from plantation owners seeking compensation — demanded that Haiti pay an indemnity of one hundred and fifty million francs as the price of diplomatic recognition. The sum was later reduced to ninety million francs, but the principle held: Haiti, the nation built by people who had liberated themselves from slavery, was required to pay reparations to the people who had enslaved them, for the loss of the property that had been the enslaved people themselves.

Haiti paid that burden — refinanced multiple times and ultimately transferred to American banks — well into the twentieth century, its development shadowed for generations by the weight of an obligation imposed on a free people as the price of their recognized freedom. The wealth extracted from the labor of enslaved people, and then extracted again as debt from the nation those people built, is the absent floor operating at its most total. No constitution. No obligation. No floor. Only the extraction continuing under new legal instruments, enforced by the diplomatic and military power of nations whose own constitutions had encoded the same absent floor.

Apply the child test to Haiti. What does the absent floor produce, not for a single child in a Wisconsin county, but for generations of children on an island whose labor built the wealth of the Western world and whose nation was then required to pay for the privilege of its own liberation?

It produces a country that in the twenty-first century remains among the poorest in the Western hemisphere — not despite its history but because of it. The absent floor, operated at scale, across generations, under the protection of international legal structures that encoded the same design choices as the Philadelphia Convention, produces exactly what the child test predicts: children with nothing, in a nation with nothing, as the compounded interest of two centuries of constitutional absence.

The founders knew this was possible. Haiti showed them in real time. They chose the walls over the floor.

THE DOCUMENT DELIVERS nothing to the child at the bottom. That is not a failure of interpretation. It is the design.

The next chapter examines how that design went further — not only withholding protection but actively using some children to generate power for the people who owned them.

3

The Arithmetic of Extraction

There is a number at the center of the American founding that no political theory produced and no philosophical argument justified. Not derived from Locke or Montesquieu. Not the conclusion of any principled debate. It is the residue of a negotiation — the number that remained when the scarcity orientations of the men in the room had finished their work on each other. The number is three-fifths.

To understand what this meant in practice: every five enslaved people — men, women, and children — were counted as three people for the purpose of deciding how many representatives a state sent to Congress. This arrangement gave Southern states more political power in proportion to their total population. The enslaved people counted in this arithmetic received nothing from it. They could not vote, hold office, or claim any protection the additional representation was meant to provide. They were counted to generate power for the people who owned them. During the August 1787 debates, delegate James Wilson of Pennsylvania put the contradiction precisely and without diplomatic softening: Are they admitted as citizens — then why are they not admitted on an equality with white citizens? Are they admitted as property — then why is not other property admitted into the computation? Wilson's question named the logic exactly. The founders were not confused about what they were doing. They were negotiating it. Wilson's question went unanswered. The compromise passed.

It is worth pausing on who else was excluded. Free women — white and Black — were counted as whole persons for apportionment, each one counted as one. But counted only. They could not vote, hold office, or participate in the government their presence helped to size. Their bodies contributed to the political arithmetic. Their voices did not enter it. The right to vote — suffrage, meaning the legal right to cast a ballot — did not extend to women until the Nineteenth Amendment was ratified in 1920, one hundred and thirty-three years after the Constitution was written. The political standing of children was never contemplated at all, not at the founding and not since. Women and children had been present in the revolution — managing farms, supplying troops, nursing the wounded, in some cases fighting. They were written out of the founding document as if they had not been there. The Preamble says we the people. The provisions defined people in ways that excluded the majority of actual human beings living in the new nation.

Article I, Section 2 used the phrase all other Persons. The document could not bring itself to say enslaved. The people counted as three-fifths to allocate political power to those who owned them are referred to, in the founding document of a nation built on the proposition that all men are created equal, as all other Persons. Three-fifths for representation. Zero for protection. Her existence in the census increased the number of congressmen from the states where she was enslaved — congressmen who would vote to maintain the system of her enslavement. She was the instrument of her own oppression's political perpetuation. That is not rhetoric. It is the arithmetic of the provision, applied literally to the child who lived under it.

TO UNDERSTAND how this provision came to exist, begin with what the abundance alternative actually proposed — because it existed, it was argued, and it lost.

The Northern delegates' position on the counting of enslaved people was not, at its core, a moral argument, though the moral argument was available and occasionally made. It was a structural argument with moral implications. Their position was this: if enslaved people are property — if the law of the Southern states defines them as such, if they have no political standing, no vote, no voice, no claim on the government — then they should not count toward that government's representation any more than a planter's horses or tobacco crop counted. You cannot simultaneously define a human being as property and then count that human being to increase the legislative power of the property owner.

The argument had internal consistency. It was made by delegates from Massachusetts, Connecticut, and New York. It was the abundance alternative — not because it was generous toward the enslaved, which it was not, but because it refused to encode the logic of extraction into the founding arithmetic. If enslaved people did not count, the Southern states would have less representation, less power, less ability to protect the institution of slavery through federal law. The absence of their counting was not justice — it was the refusal to compound injustice by making the enslaved people instruments of their own oppression's political survival.

The Southern states' position was simpler and more naked. They wanted the numbers. Full counting of the enslaved population would give the South — Virginia especially, with its enormous enslaved population — a dominant position in the House of Representatives and therefore in the Electoral College. This was not a principled argument about the nature of personhood. It was a demand for leverage. The South needed the count because the count meant power.

Between those two positions, the negotiation produced three-fifths. Not from principle. From the arithmetic of what each side needed to stay at the table. The number is not a compromise between two moral positions. It is the residue of two scarcity orientations — Northern fear of Southern legislative dominance, Southern demand for the representation their enslaved population could generate — grinding against each other until the minimum viable agreement emerged.

James Wilson of Pennsylvania, who had argued strenuously against counting enslaved people at all, accepted three-fifths because the alternative was the convention's collapse. Gouverneur Morris, also of Pennsylvania, gave perhaps the most honest assessment of what was happening: he said he would never concur in upholding domestic slavery, but he would do anything consistent to save the nation. The nation was saved. The arithmetic was encoded. The child was counted as three-fifths.

WHAT DOES IT MEAN — clinically, precisely, without rhetorical amplification — to be counted as three-fifths of a person?

It means your existence is acknowledged by the document. You are not invisible to it. The document sees you — sees you clearly enough to count you, to include you in its arithmetic. But the counting serves a purpose that is the opposite of protection. Your presence in the census increases the power of the people whose interest is in your continued subjugation. You are counted in, and simultaneously counted out. Included in the arithmetic of power, excluded from the arithmetic of rights.

The child born into slavery in South Carolina in 1789 was, under this provision, a political instrument. Three-fifths of her body generated a fraction of a representative. That representative would vote in the Congress of the United States — would vote on the laws governing the slave trade, on the fugitive slave provisions, on the western expansion of slavery into new territories, on every federal question that bore on whether she would live and die in chains. Her counted fraction supported the political apparatus that maintained her condition.

The child test applied here is not sentimental. It is mathematical. The provision produces a child whose existence is simultaneously recognized and weaponized. The document sees her. It uses her. It protects her not at all.

This is what dehumanization looks like when it is encoded rather than merely practiced. The scarcity orientation, confronted with the moral problem of extraction, does not resolve it through moral reasoning. It resolves it through arithmetic. Reduce the person to a fraction and the fraction to a political instrument, and the fact of her full humanity need never be directly confronted. The room did not debate whether the enslaved child was a person. It debated what fraction of her personhood would be administratively useful. That is the clinical signature of institutionalized dehumanization: the question of humanity is replaced by the question of utility, and the replacement is so complete that the original question stops being asked.

Dehumanize and you self-devour. The epigraph states the verdict. This chapter documents the mechanism.

This is the founding bias at its most structural. Not the absence of a floor, which Chapter Two examined. The active use of the person at the bottom to generate power for the person at the top. The absent floor is a failure of obligation. The three-fifths compromise is something more precise: it is the encoding of extraction as representation.

CHAPTER TWO EXAMINED Haiti as what happens when the absent floor operates at civilizational scale — the laboratory of a population pushed below the minimum threshold of human sustainability, revolting, and then being made to pay for its own liberation.

The three-fifths compromise and the Haitian Revolution are two faces of the same founding logic, and they must be examined together to understand what that logic fully was.

The Haitian Revolution began in 1791 — four years after the Philadelphia Convention encoded the three-fifths compromise into the American Constitution. The timing is not coincidental. The founding decade of the American republic was also the decade in which the largest and most profitable slave society in the Western hemisphere was violently dismantled by the people it had been built on. The men who wrote the Constitution in 1787 and argued for its ratification in 1788 were governing the new republic in 1791 when the Haitian uprising began. They watched it unfold in real time.

What they saw was the three-fifths logic taken to its global conclusion. Saint-Domingue had applied the arithmetic of extraction at maximum scale — five hundred thousand enslaved people generating wealth for approximately thirty thousand free colonists, with no floor, no protection, no claim, no count except as property. The result was not political imbalance. It was revolution. The people at the bottom, extracted to the point of absolute destitution, did what the child test predicts they would do: they took by force what the document had refused to provide by obligation.

The American founders' response to Haiti reveals what they understood the three-fifths compromise to be. If the compromise had been, in their minds, a regrettable transitional arrangement — a temporary encoding of an institution they expected to wither — their response to the Haitian Revolution would have been different. They might have seen it as confirmation that the institution was unsustainable and must be addressed. Instead, they saw it as a threat to be contained. The Haitian example was not a warning that the three-fifths logic would eventually produce revolt. It was a demonstration that it already had — ninety miles from the coast of the United States, in a colony whose enslaved population was proportionally far larger than America's but whose logic of extraction was identical.

Thomas Jefferson, who wrote that all men are created equal and owned over six hundred enslaved people across his lifetime, was President when Haiti declared independence in 1804. His response was to impose a trade embargo and refuse recognition. The Haitian Revolution was not, in Jefferson's framework, the vindication of the Declaration's principles. It was the nightmare that the three-fifths compromise had been designed to forestall — the arithmetic of extraction producing its inevitable human consequence, and that consequence arriving with guns.

The connection between the three-fifths compromise and Haiti is therefore not merely historical context. It is the clinical demonstration that the founders knew, in the decade of the Constitution's ratification, exactly what the arithmetic of extraction produced when pushed to its limit. They saw it. They understood it. And they responded not by examining the arithmetic but by quarantining the example — refusing recognition, closing ports, suppressing the Haitian story in public discourse — because the example, if widely circulated and honestly understood, threatened the stability of the system the three-fifths compromise was designed to protect.

The child in Saint-Domingue and the child in South Carolina were produced by the same logic. The three-fifths compromise was the American encoding of that logic. Haiti was its global crystallization. They are not separate stories. They are the same story, told in two registers.

THE THREE-FIFTHS COMPROMISE was formally abolished by the Fourteenth Amendment in 1868, eighty-one years after it was encoded. The Fourteenth Amendment replaced it with a provision counting the whole number of persons in each state, excluding Indians not taxed. The fractional arithmetic was repudiated. The formerly enslaved — now freed, now nominally citizens — would be counted as whole persons. But counting as a whole person for representation and having the right to vote — suffrage, the legal right to cast a ballot and participate in choosing representatives — are different things. The Fourteenth Amendment guaranteed the first. The second remained denied by force, by law, and by systematic terror for another century.

The repudiation was real. It was also, immediately and systematically, undermined by the mechanisms the document's design made available.

The Fourteenth Amendment counted formerly enslaved people as whole persons for the purpose of representation. It did not — could not, under the constitutional architecture Chapter Two examined — guarantee them the right to vote, the right to hold office, the right to equal protection in practice rather than in principle. The Southern states retained their representatives, now calculated on the full population count, while simultaneously erecting the apparatus of Jim Crow — literacy tests, poll taxes, grandfather clauses, white primaries, and the systematic violence of the Ku Klux Klan — to prevent the newly counted persons from exercising the political power their counting was supposed to represent.

The result was a precise inversion of the three-fifths compromise, equally extractive in its logic. Under the three-fifths compromise, Black bodies generated three-fifths of a representative for the white men who owned them. Under the post-Reconstruction system, Black bodies generated a full representative for the white men who disenfranchised them. The fraction changed. The extraction continued. The political power generated by Black population was captured by white political structures in both cases. The arithmetic of extraction had been updated, not ended.

The Fourteenth Amendment changed the fraction. The template remained. Some bodies continue to generate political power for others, without sharing in the power their presence creates.

TRACE that logic into the present, because the child test requires it.

Modern redistricting — the drawing of legislative district lines after each decennial census — is the direct institutional descendant of the three-fifths compromise's central question: which people count, and for whose benefit? The question has never been settled. It has only been renegotiated in each generation, using the tools available to the people with the power to draw the lines.

Gerrymandering — the practice of drawing district lines to maximize the political power of one group at the expense of another — is the three-fifths logic in contemporary form. It does not require explicit racial arithmetic. It achieves the same result through geographic precision: concentrating minority voters into a small number of districts where their votes produce few representatives, or dispersing them across many districts where their votes produce none. The body is counted in the census. The vote is neutralized in the district map. Counted in. Counted out. The template is 1787.

The census methodology debates of the twenty-first century are equally direct descendants. The question of whether to count undocumented immigrants in the census — which determines both congressional apportionment and federal funding allocation — is structurally identical to the three-fifths debate. One side argues that the people are here, that they contribute to the economy, that they should be counted for representation. The other side argues that people without legal standing should not generate political power for the jurisdictions where they live. The arguments have different content than 1787. The architecture is the same.

The Supreme Court's 2019 decision in Rucho v. Common Cause, holding that federal courts cannot review partisan gerrymandering claims, is the DeShaney of redistricting — the jurisprudential confirmation that the constitutional architecture, as designed, provides no remedy for the systematic manipulation of political arithmetic along demographic lines. The document does not prohibit extraction. It provides no floor of representational equity. The child born in a gerrymandered district inherits the political arithmetic of her geography, which was drawn by people whose interest was in preventing her counted presence from generating political power for her community.

The Voting Rights Act of 1965 was the legislative attempt to provide what the constitutional architecture withheld — an affirmative obligation on the state to protect the political rights of populations the three-fifths logic had historically disenfranchised. The Supreme Court's 2013 decision in Shelby County v. Holder gutted the Act's preclearance provision — the requirement that jurisdictions with histories of voting discrimination obtain federal approval before changing their voting laws. Chief Justice Roberts, writing for the majority, held that the conditions that justified preclearance in 1965 no longer existed.

Within twenty-four hours of the Shelby County decision, several states began implementing voting restrictions that the preclearance requirement had previously blocked.

The child test applied to Shelby County: what does it produce for the child whose community has a documented history of voting discrimination, in a state that has just been freed from the requirement to justify its voting law changes to federal reviewers?

It produces the same child the three-fifths compromise produced. Counted. Present. Generating the representation arithmetic of her district. And systematically prevented from exercising the political power her counted presence is supposed to create.

THE INCARCERATION DIMENSION of this structural legacy requires specific attention, because it is the most direct contemporary expression of the three-fifths template.

The United States incarcerates a higher proportion of its population than any other nation on earth. Approximately two million people are in prison or jail at any given moment. The racial disparity in that population is well documented: Black Americans, who constitute approximately thirteen percent of the national population, constitute approximately forty percent of the prison population.

Incarcerated people are counted in the census at the location of their incarceration, not their home communities. This practice — known as prison gerrymandering — means that predominantly white rural counties, which house large prisons, gain population count and therefore political representation from the bodies of predominantly Black and brown people from urban communities who cannot vote in the jurisdictions where they are counted. The bodies generate representation. The people whose bodies are counted receive none of the political power their presence creates.

The template is 1787. The fraction has changed — incarcerated people are counted as whole persons, not three-fifths. But the logic is identical: bodies from one community, counted to generate political power for another community, with no reciprocal benefit flowing to the people whose bodies are doing the counting work.

The child test applied to prison gerrymandering: the child whose parent is incarcerated in a rural county two hundred miles from home contributes to that county's congressional apportionment and state legislative representation. Her home community, from which the incarcerated parent has been removed, loses that population count and its associated political weight. She grows up in a community that has been politically diminished by the removal of its members, while those members' bodies generate representation in a community that did not produce them and to which they will not return.

This is the arithmetic of extraction operating in the twenty-first century, under a Constitution whose Fourteenth Amendment formally abolished the three-fifths fraction but whose architecture provided no mechanism to prevent the extraction logic from finding new instruments.

SHE IS THREE-FIFTHS. She is also whole. The document chose which of those truths to encode.

The next chapter examines the man who articulated the abundance alternative most clearly, narrowed it most consequentially, and signed the document that encoded neither truth fully.

Dehumanize and you self-devour.
— RNB

after countless impossibilities,
I am here after infinite challenges,
carrying more wisdom in me
than all that exists in the world.

Dehumanize me,
you destroy yourself and your future.
You who is also me —
need not be so afraid,
so greedy,
so one-sided,
so empty,
so scarce,
when you are abundance incarnate.

Remember —
you already have it all.
Kill others and you kill yourself.
The cycle of scarcity devours you,
undoubtedly.
Dehumanize and it compounds.

Your agency, your gift,
is to create — to find meaningful solutions —
but never dehumanize,
no matter how afraid,
no matter how empty it feels.

You are not empty. You never were.

4

The Narrowing

James Madison arrived in Philadelphia in May 1787 as the most prepared man in the room. He had spent months in systematic study — reading everything available on the history of confederacies, ancient and modern, constructing a theory of republican government more sophisticated than anything his contemporaries had produced. His conclusion was clear: the Articles had failed because they created a government acting on states rather than on individuals. A government without that direct reach could not tax, could not enforce, could not govern. The solution was a genuinely national government with broad authority to act for the general welfare of the union — powerful enough to serve the people who lived under it, not merely to manage the states that contained them. Read through the child test, this vision produces a government with the authority and the obligation to provide the conditions of a child's development. Not a government that merely refrains from harming her. One that acts on her behalf. That government was what Madison brought to the room. What emerged from the room was something different. And what Madison then did with what emerged is the clinical subject of this chapter.

THE NARROWING HAPPENED in three movements. The first was structural: the Great Compromise replaced Madison's proportional Senate with equal state representation. Madison fought this and lost. The Senate was built to protect state sovereignty rather than serve individual welfare, and a chamber organized around sovereignty will always be more responsive to the governments it represents than to the people those governments contain. The second movement was substantive: the broad general welfare language of the Virginia Plan was replaced by an enumerated powers structure, with the general welfare phrase reduced to a taxing and spending authorization rather than a freestanding national mandate. The abundance obligation became a permission. The government could choose to provide. It was not required to. The third movement was the most consequential — and it happened after the convention ended.

MADISON LEFT Philadelphia in September 1787 having lost most of what he most wanted. The national veto over state laws was gone. The proportional Senate was gone. The broad general welfare mandate was gone. What remained was a document he believed was insufficient to the problems it was meant to solve — he said so explicitly to Jefferson, in letters written in the weeks after the convention. He feared the Constitution would neither effectually answer its national object nor prevent the local mischiefs that had made the existing system unworkable.

Then the ratification fight began. And Madison made a choice.

He could have maintained his position — argued publicly that the document was inadequate, that the general welfare clause needed to be understood broadly, that the national government required genuine authority to act for the people who lived under it. He did not. Instead, he became the document's most sophisticated defender. In The Federalist Papers, co-written with Hamilton and Jay, Madison argued not for what he had wanted but for what existed. And in doing so, he completed the narrowing he had failed to prevent in the room.

The critical moment is Federalist 41, published in January 1788. Madison is defending the Taxing and Spending Clause against Anti-Federalist critics who fear that the general welfare language grants unlimited power to Congress. His argument, made to reassure those critics, is that the general welfare phrase is merely a summary heading for the specific enumerated powers that follow it — that the expansive language means only what the specific list permits.

This argument was not forced on Madison. It was not the only available reading of the clause. Hamilton, his co-author, would later argue precisely the opposite — that the general welfare language was a freestanding grant of authority, broader than the enumerated list. The two interpretations were both plausible. Madison chose the narrower one. He chose it under the political pressure of ratification, in the service of calming fears that the national government would become too powerful.

The abundance vision that Madison had brought to Philadelphia — the government with broad authority to serve the general welfare — was narrowed in the convention by the defended positions of other men. Then it was narrowed again, in Federalist 41, by Madison himself.

MADISON WAS NOT ACTING in bad faith. He was a man of extraordinary intelligence and genuine public commitment who had been through something — the revolution, the failed confederation, the brutal negotiation of the convention — that had reorganized his judgment in ways he could not fully see. The trauma of watching what he believed was a workable system of government come apart had produced in him a specific form of defensive pragmatism: the willingness to accept a lesser document and then defend it as sufficient, because the alternative — continued constitutional failure — felt unsurvivable.

The clinical framework names this precisely. It is what happens when a person with an abundance vision encounters the scarcity orientation of a group under pressure. The vision does not disappear. It is not replaced by cynicism. It is progressively subordinated to the practical requirements of what the group can agree to, and then — in the most psychologically complex move — the person who held the vision becomes the most articulate defender of the agreement that diminished it. Not because he has abandoned the vision. Because the defended position has been internalized as the best available approximation of what the vision required.

But Chapter One's deeper clinical layer applies here too. Madison was not only a traumatized man under pressure. He was a man formed inside the monarchical system, who had identified with his aggressors sufficiently to reproduce their structural logic in the document he helped create. The Virginia Plan's broad national authority was the abundance vision. The Federalist 41 narrowing was the monarch's instinct — to concentrate interpretive authority in the hands of those who already held it, to ensure that the general welfare clause would serve the propertied, the powerful, the people already in the room, rather than obligating the system to the child who had no voice in it.

Madison spent the rest of his life managing this internalization. His constitutional positions shifted across the decades — nationalist in 1787, states-rightist by the 1790s, somewhere between the two positions late in his life. He revised his convention notes. He deferred their publication until after his death, in 1836, because he feared that showing what he had originally proposed and what he had accepted would be used against him. He was right to fear it. The gap between what he brought to Philadelphia and what he signed in September 1787, and then defended in January 1788, is the founding bias made visible in a single biography.

What was narrowed in that biography was not merely a constitutional provision. It was the obligation to the child. The government that Madison had originally envisioned would have been the constitutional basis for the floors every child requires. The government that emerged from the narrowing — authorized but not obligated, empowered but not duty-bound — left those floors absent.

And the argument Madison made in Federalist 41, defending that absence as constitutional design rather than constitutional failure, became the interpretive foundation on which two centuries of courts would deny that the absent floor was a problem the Constitution was required to address.

DeShaney is Federalist 41's endpoint. The child is Madison's narrowing made flesh.

THE NARROWING WAS DESIGNED to protect a specific population from the obligations of national government. It succeeded. But the child test requires that we follow the consequences not only to the populations the scarcity orientation most visibly failed — the enslaved, the formally excluded, those the document counted and did not protect — but to the populations the scarcity orientation believed it was protecting.

The deaths of despair data forces that examination.

The term was coined by economists Anne Case and Angus Deaton in research published in 2015 and developed in their 2020 book of the same name. Their finding was stark: beginning in the 1990s and accelerating through the first two decades of the twenty-first century, mortality rates for middle-aged white Americans without college degrees began rising — an almost unprecedented reversal in a wealthy nation during peacetime. The causes were three: drug overdose, alcohol-related liver disease, and suicide. These are the deaths of despair — not deaths from disease or accident or the ordinary attrition of aging, but deaths from the accumulated weight of lives that had become unbearable.

The populations most affected were rural, non-college-educated, predominantly white. They were the demographic that the constitutional architecture had, in the framing of its defenders, been designed to protect. The small states whose equal Senate representation the Great Compromise guaranteed. The property-owning yeomanry that the founders imagined as the republic's backbone.

The people for whom the scarcity orientation of the Philadelphia Convention had constructed its defensive architecture.

By 2020, the mortality gap between white Americans without college degrees and those with college degrees had grown to levels that had no modern precedent in wealthy nations. Life expectancy for this population was declining while life expectancy for college-educated Americans continued to rise. The United States had produced, within its borders, two populations with diverging biological futures — not separated primarily by race, though race remained a powerful predictor, but separated by education and the economic security that education had increasingly come to represent.

The child test applied to deaths of despair: what does the constitutional architecture produce, in the long run, for the child born into a community whose economic foundation has been removed, whose social fabric has frayed, whose parents are dying at historic rates from suicide and addiction, and who has no constitutional right to the healthcare, education, or economic security that might interrupt the cycle?

It produces the next generation of deaths of despair. The absent floor is not a problem that stabilizes. It compounds. Each generation that grows up without the conditions of development produces a next generation more vulnerable to the same absence. The scarcity orientation, encoded in the founding document and defended across two centuries as constitutional principle, eventually consumes the population it was designed to protect.

This is what Madison's narrowing produces at its furthest downstream reach. Not only the child in South Carolina, counted as three-fifths. Not only Joshua DeShaney, beaten while the caseworkers watched. But the white man in West Virginia or Ohio or rural Pennsylvania, dying at fifty-two from an opioid overdose in a community where the mill closed twenty years ago and the hospital closed last year and the constitutional architecture provides no floor beneath either loss.

The deaths of despair are not a policy failure. They are a constitutional outcome — what you get, across enough generations, when the founding document authorizes general welfare and obligates nothing.

THE SCARCITY ORIENTATION encoded at the founding does not merely fail to provide abundance. It produces scarcity — in the developmental conditions available to children, in the social trust available to communities, in the biological capacity of populations to sustain themselves. The document designed to protect a population from the obligations of shared welfare eventually produces the conditions that make that population unable to survive.

Dehumanize and you self-devour. The founders dehumanized through arithmetic and through absence — through the three-fifths fraction and through the general welfare that was authorized but never obligated. They were themselves dehumanized in the process: men who had identified with their aggressors so completely that they could not see what they were reproducing, who had suppressed the parts of their own experience that the monarchy required them to suppress, who had become — in the closed room, under pressure, defending the minimum viable agreement — the monarchs they had just defeated, distributing among themselves the authority they had fought to reclaim.

That is the founding bias at its deepest level. Not merely a scarcity orientation winning the close calls. The identification with the aggressor encoding the aggressor's logic into the document of liberation. The peace treaty passing that logic forward, generation after generation, crystallized and protected by its own immune system, as the definition of normal.

Friedrich Nietzsche's concept of revaluation addresses precisely this condition. When the values a civilization has encoded produce outcomes that destroy the civilization — when the document of liberation produces the conditions it was meant to prevent — what is required is not reform. Not the addition of corrective policies within the existing value framework. Revaluation: the examination of the values themselves, the willingness to name the pathology before proposing what replaces it.

The child's voice performs this revaluation at its most irreducible level. She does not argue with Federalist 41. She does not dispute the originalist interpretation of the Taxing and Spending Clause. She presents her body and its needs and the question that the Preamble itself announced: are the blessings of liberty secured to her posterity? The document says they should be. The provisions say they need not be. The gap between those two statements is what two and a half centuries of children have fallen into.

The revaluation begins with seeing that gap clearly. Chapter Five examines why clarity has been so difficult to achieve — the immune system the document built for itself, the mechanisms by which the defended position protects itself from reexamination across generations. After that, the comparative evidence of Part Two will show what constitutional moments organized around the abundance orientation have produced instead. And Part Three will ask, with the full weight of the diagnosis behind it, what clarity — at last — makes possible.

The child is still standing there. She has been standing there since September 17, 1787. Posterity, holding the Preamble's promise and the provisions' silence, waiting for the document to close the gap its own mission statement requires.

5

The Immune System

Every pathology develops defenses. The Constitution's scarcity orientation — the absent floor, the arithmetic of extraction, the narrowing of general welfare into permission rather than obligation — did not survive two and a half centuries by accident. It survived because the document that encoded it also encoded the mechanisms to protect it from being changed.

BEGIN with what is being protected and why the protection was necessary. The men who left Philadelphia in September 1787 knew the document was a compromise. The Anti-Federalists — Patrick Henry, George Mason, the writers who published under the name Brutus — argued that it concentrated too much power in the federal government and would inevitably serve the wealthy rather than the common man. They were partly right. And the founders knew it.

The Bill of Rights — the first ten amendments, ratified in 1791 — was the price of ratification. Without the promise of explicit protections for speech, religion, assembly, and the rights of the accused, enough states would have refused to ratify. Madison, who had originally opposed a bill of rights as unnecessary, drafted one in the first Congress because the alternative was failure.

The Bill of Rights is real. Its protections have mattered enormously. But notice what it protects: individuals from the government's power to act against them. Freedom of speech. Protection from unreasonable search. The right to a fair trial. What it does not protect — what it was never designed to protect — is the individual from the government's failure to act for them. The First Amendment protects your right to speak. It does not protect your child's right to eat. The Bill of Rights added a roof and walls to a building that had no floor. The child at the bottom was now protected from the government coming through her door. She was still unprotected from everything she needed that the government was not required to provide. This is what the immune system was built to preserve: the specific design choice made in Philadelphia — to authorize general welfare without obligating it, to protect liberty without guaranteeing its conditions.

THE LIVING DOCUMENT claim must be examined here because it is the immune system's most effective disguise. The Constitution, its defenders say, adapts to changing times through judicial interpretation and the amendment process. It does not need to be rewritten because it was designed to evolve. This claim is both true and false, and the way it is both at once is precisely what makes it so effective as a defense.

It is true that the Constitution has changed. Twenty-seven amendments have been added since 1787 — the abolition of slavery, women's suffrage, the direct election of senators. These are real changes. But it is false that the document was designed to evolve freely. Article V was deliberately constructed to make change extraordinarily difficult. Two-thirds of both houses of Congress must approve any proposed amendment. Then three-quarters of states — currently thirty-eight of fifty — must ratify it. The thirteen least populous states represent roughly four percent of the American population. Those thirteen states can block any amendment supported by the other ninety-six percent. A change with overwhelming national support can be permanently blocked by states containing one in twenty-five Americans.

This is not an accident. The founders understood that the defended positions encoded in the document — equal Senate representation, the property protections, the absence of affirmative obligations — would face future challenges. They built the amendment process to ensure those challenges could not easily succeed. The living document claim obscures this. It tells the child inheriting the absent floor that change is possible, that the process exists. What it does not tell her is that the process was engineered to require a level of consensus that almost nothing in a polarized democracy can achieve — and that the provisions most in need of change are protected by the very states whose power depends on them remaining unchanged.

The Senate's equal state representation is the clearest example. It is the provision that most directly encodes the small states' scarcity orientation into the legislative architecture — producing the chamber that most reliably blocks affirmative legislation on healthcare, education, and the floors that an obligated general welfare would require. And it is protected by the most extraordinary clause in Article V: no state shall be deprived of its equal suffrage in the Senate without its consent. The one provision that most needs to change cannot be changed unless the states that benefit from it agree to give it up. The people who won the close call in 1787 wrote into the document a guarantee that they could never lose it again without their own permission.

THE JUDICIAL INTERPRETATION mechanism is subtler but equally effective. Because the amendment process is so difficult, constitutional change has largely happened through the courts. The Supreme Court's interpretation of provisions has evolved substantially — expanding rights in some eras, contracting them in others.

This is what the living document claim most often points to: the courts keep the document current. What this mechanism actually produces is constitutional change controlled by nine unelected judges appointed for life, whose interpretations can be reversed by subsequent courts, and whose decisions reflect the political composition of the presidents and senates that appointed them. The child at the bottom has no vote in this process. She has no lobby. She cannot fund the litigation that reaches the Supreme Court or the campaigns that shape its composition.

DeShaney v. Winnebago County — the 1989 case examined in Chapter Two, in which the Supreme Court ruled that the Constitution imposed no duty on the state to protect a child it had been monitoring from his abusive father — is this mechanism applied directly to the child test. Chief Justice Rehnquist's majority held that the Constitution's protections run only against what the government does to you, not what it fails to do for you. Justice Brennan's dissent argued that once the state inserted itself into Joshua's situation, it assumed a responsibility it could not simply abandon. The majority's reading prevailed — not because it was the only available reading, but because it maintained the absent floor that the document's architecture was built to protect. The living document interpreted Joshua DeShaney out of its protection. The amendment process provided no remedy. The immune system worked as designed.

ARTICLE V IS the mechanism's centerpiece. Two paths to amendment — both requiring supermajorities at every stage. The congressional path requires two-thirds of the House, two-thirds of the Senate, and three-fourths of the states. The convention path, never successfully used, requires two-thirds of state legislatures to call it and three-fourths to ratify what it produces. In practice, only twenty-seven amendments have been ratified in two hundred and thirty-five years. Ten came immediately as the Bill of Rights. Of the remaining seventeen, several corrected catastrophic failures — slavery, women's suffrage — after social upheaval made the political cost of not amending higher than the cost of amending. None added affirmative socioeconomic rights. None created a constitutional floor beneath the child at the bottom.

Before naming what the immune system costs, its genuine functions deserve honest acknowledgment. The difficulty of amendment is not only a liability. It has prevented real abuses — the elimination of presidential term limits in moments of popular enthusiasm for a particular leader, the removal of free speech protections during wartime panic, the dismantling of rights that majorities have periodically wanted to revoke. The founders' fear of faction was not paranoid. History has confirmed it repeatedly. The reverence that ordinary citizens feel for the document — the pride of standing before it, the sense that it represents something worth protecting — is not false or manipulated. It is a genuine relationship with genuine achievements.

This book does not ask anyone to surrender that relationship or deny those achievements. It asks something more precise: to notice that the immune system protecting those achievements protects everything else with equal force. It cannot distinguish between what should be preserved and what should change. The same mechanism that prevents a demagogue from rewriting the First Amendment also prevents the constitutional obligation to a hungry child from ever being established. The same amendment threshold that protects presidential term limits also protects equal Senate representation — the provision that most reliably blocks the affirmative legislation the people at the bottom require. The reverence is real. What it has been recruited to protect is larger than what it was formed around. That is not a flaw in the feeling. It is a flaw in the mechanism the feeling has been made to serve.

The founders called this stability. It is stability of a particular kind — the stability of a document that encodes the scarcity orientation and then makes that encoding nearly permanent. Madison argued in Federalist 49 against frequent revision on the grounds that public veneration of the document was necessary for republican government to function. He was not wrong that veneration is useful. He did not acknowledge that what was being venerated included the defended positions that his own vision had failed to overcome. Franklin's warning — a republic, if you can keep it — pointed to external threats. The more serious threat was internal: that the document designed to sustain the republic would also sustain the arrangements that prevented the republic from delivering on its own Preamble. Article V ensures that those arrangements are the most protected things in it. The immune system does not distinguish between what should be preserved and what should be changed. It preserves everything with equal ferocity.

THE CRYSTALLIZATION IS NOW COMPLETE. The Prologue described the Constitution as a trauma document — a peace treaty encoding the defended positions of men whose nervous systems had been reorganized by revolution. The previous chapters documented what those provisions produced: the absent floor, the arithmetic of extraction, the narrowing of general welfare into authorization without obligation. This chapter has shown how those provisions protect themselves — through the living document myth that obscures how difficult change actually is, through the judicial mechanism that makes constitutional evolution dependent on courts shaped by the same political processes the document governs, and through Article V, which requires the people who benefited from the close calls to consent to losing them.

The child does not inherit only the absent floor. She does not inherit only the arithmetic of extraction. She inherits the system designed to prevent both from being addressed. She is born into a household whose rules were written by a traumatized ancestor, handed down as sacred, and made deliberately resistant to change. She cannot vote in the Senate race that shapes the court that interprets the document that governs the floor she does not have. She is downstream of every mechanism this chapter has examined. And she is the measure by which every one of those mechanisms must finally be judged.

Part One has performed the diagnosis. The founding trauma.

The provisions it produced. The immune system that protects those provisions across generations. The record is clear. Part Two now asks what other founding moments produced when the child test was operative — even imperfectly, even incompletely — at the founding. What documents were written by people who had experienced what it means to have no floor, and who encoded that experience into affirmative obligation rather than negative liberty. The comparison is not offered to condemn the American founding. It is offered because diagnosis without comparative evidence is incomplete. You cannot fully see what a design produces until you have seen what a different design produces instead.

Part II

6

The Liberation Documents

Every constitution is written by people who have experienced something. The American founders experienced revolution and built accordingly — a government that could not harm you directly, that checked its own power carefully, that left the general welfare to the political process rather than obligating it in the document itself. Their experience was specific: men who had fought a distant crown, who feared what concentrated power could do, and who could not see — from inside that experience — that the concentrated power most likely to harm the child at the bottom was not the tyrannical state but the absent one.

The South African framers of 1996 experienced something different. They had lived under apartheid — a system so total that it classified human beings by race, assigned them to geographical bantustans, denied them citizenship in the country of their birth, controlled where they could live, work, travel, and be buried, and maintained all of this through systematic violence for nearly half a century. When they sat down to write a constitution, they knew from direct experience what happens to human beings when the state has no obligation to recognize their dignity. They built the opposite. The German framers of 1949 had watched a constitutional democracy

— the Weimar Republic, with its sophisticated rights protections and representative legislature — vote itself into fascism. They had seen procedural rights used to destroy the very order those rights were meant to protect. When they wrote the Basic Law, their organizing question was not how to limit state power but how to prevent that specific catastrophe from ever happening again. These two documents are the sharpest available contrast to the American founding — not because they are perfect, but because they were written by people whose experience produced the opposite constitutional instinct. Where the American founders feared the state and built protections against its power to act, these framers feared the state's failure to act and built obligations into the document itself. The child finds something different here. It finds a floor.

THE SOUTH AFRICAN Constitution came into force in February 1997, replacing the interim document that had governed the country's transition from apartheid. Its drafting was deliberately public — more than two million submissions from ordinary citizens, public hearings across the country, a process designed so that the people most excluded from every previous governing document in South African history could see themselves in the new one. Article 10 states it plainly: every person has inherent dignity and the right to have their dignity respected and protected.

That sentence is the abundance floor in its simplest form. Not a limitation on what the state may do to you. An affirmative statement about what every person is, and what the state is therefore required to respect. Dignity is not earned. It is not conditional on race, property, or political standing. It inheres. The state's obligation follows from the person's existence. Compare this to the American document. The Preamble announces that the government exists to promote the general welfare and secure the blessings of liberty to posterity. Then the provisions create no affirmative obligation to the child's dignity, development, or survival. DeShaney confirmed what those provisions actually deliver: the state need not protect you from harm it did not directly cause. An American child's dignity is not constitutionally recognized. It is hoped for in the Preamble and left to the political process to provide or withhold.

The South African Constitution does not stop at dignity. Section 26 establishes the right to adequate housing. Section 27 establishes the right to healthcare, sufficient food and water, and social security. Section 29 establishes the right to a basic education. Section 28 — the provision that speaks most directly to any child — enumerates what every child is entitled to: a name and nationality from birth; family or appropriate alternative care; basic nutrition, shelter, healthcare, and social services; protection from maltreatment, neglect, abuse, and degradation; protection from exploitative labor. These are not aspirations. They are enforceable constitutional obligations. A child in South Africa can bring a claim in court if the state fails to provide basic nutrition. There is no equivalent provision in the American Constitution. No constitutional right to basic nutrition, shelter, or basic healthcare for an American child. No right to protection from the neglect of state institutions responsible for her welfare. Joshua DeShaney had no constitutional claim when the caseworkers watched and did nothing, because the American document contains nothing equivalent to Section 28. One document produces a child whose dignity is recognized, whose basic needs are constitutionally obligated, and who has legal recourse when the state fails. The other produces Joshua DeShaney.

IT WOULD BE dishonest not to say this: the South African Constitution has not delivered everything it promises. South Africa remains one of the most unequal societies on earth. Children still go hungry. The state's capacity to fulfill its obligations is limited by poverty, corruption, and the enormous inequality that apartheid produced and that three decades of post-apartheid governance have not fully resolved. But this is a different failure than the American failure. When the South African state fails to provide basic nutrition to a child, that failure can be named as a constitutional violation and brought before a court. When the American state fails to provide basic nutrition to a child, no constitutional violation has occurred. One failure is a broken promise. The other is a promise that was never made. A broken promise can be enforced. An unmade promise cannot. The child in South Africa has a floor to stand on even when the state fails to deliver. The American child has no floor.

~

GERMANY'S BASIC LAW — the Grundgesetz, meaning the foundational law — was adopted on May 23, 1949, four years after the collapse of the Nazi regime. It was written by people haunted by a specific memory: the Weimar Republic, Germany's first democratic constitution, had been dismantled through its own legal procedures. Article 48 of the Weimar Constitution allowed the President to rule by emergency decree. The Enabling Act of 1933, passed by the Reichstag — Germany's parliament — with the required two-thirds majority, gave Hitler's cabinet power to enact laws without parliamentary approval. The constitutional machinery was used, legally and procedurally, to destroy the constitutional order. The people who wrote the Basic Law were determined this would not happen again.

The result is a document organized around one central conviction that nothing can override: the state exists to protect human dignity. Article 1, Paragraph 1 states it directly: Human dignity shall be inviolable. To respect and protect it shall be the duty of all state authority. Dignity is not merely protected — it is beyond the reach of any law, any government, any constitutional amendment. And Article 1 is one of the provisions that cannot be amended at all. The German framers decided that some commitments must be placed beyond democratic revision entirely. This is the opposite instinct from Article V of the American Constitution. Article V protects the defended positions of 1787 by making them difficult to change. Article 1 of the Basic Law protects every person's dignity by making it impossible to remove. Both are immune systems. They protect different things.

The Basic Law also establishes what Germans call the Sozialstaatsprinzip — the social state principle, meaning the state's constitutional obligation to maintain basic social welfare for all its citizens. Article 20 declares Germany a democratic and social federal state. That word social carries constitutional weight: Germany's Federal Constitutional Court has interpreted it to mean the state cannot withdraw from the basic conditions of human life and call that freedom. Liberty without the material conditions that make it meaningful is not liberty. It is the rhetoric of liberty applied to people who lack its substance. The child who cannot be fed, housed, or educated is not free. She is simply unprotected by a government that has learned to use the language of freedom to describe her abandonment. In 2010, Germany's Federal Constitutional Court delivered a ruling that shows exactly what happens when the dignity floor is constitutionally enforced. The government had calculated welfare benefits without constitutional rigor. The Court ruled this violated the Existenzminimum — the constitutional minimum of subsistence, which the Court held covers not just food and shelter but participation in cultural life. Benefits were ordered to increase. By 2024, the monthly benefit had risen from €449 to €563 — a 25 percent gain — directly improving the lives of 6.7 million people, including 1.7 million children. This is what an enforceable floor produces: a court ruling that moves real money to real children because the constitution requires it, not because the political weather permitted it.

TWO FOUNDING TRAUMAS. Two constitutional documents. Two completely different answers to the same question. The comparison does not require declaring the American Constitution irredeemable or these documents perfect. It requires only this: the choice was available. Other founding moments made it. The American founders were not uniquely callous or uniquely blind. They were people whose specific experience produced a specific constitutional instinct. The South African and German framers had different experiences and produced different instincts. The founding trauma shapes the document. The document shapes what the child inherits. That is not destiny. It is a choice made under specific conditions — and other conditions have produced other choices. The next chapter examines what those choices look like when societies build constitutional cultures organized around the abundance orientation not in the aftermath of catastrophe but as a steady, generational commitment to the child the Preamble always promised to protect.

7

The Welfare Constitutions

There is a question that comes up whenever the Nordic countries enter a conversation about what government can provide. It goes like this: yes, but those are small homogeneous societies. You cannot compare them to the United States. The question deserves a direct answer. Norway has a population of five million. Finland four and a half million. Sweden ten million. The United States has three hundred and thirty million. These are real differences in scale. The homogeneity point is more complicated — all three Nordic countries have significant immigrant populations and have become considerably more diverse over the past thirty years — but the scale objection is fair.

Here is what it does not explain. The child poverty rate in the United States is roughly four times higher than in Finland. American children are more likely to die before their fifth birthday than children in any other wealthy nation. These gaps are not explained by population size. Norway is small. So is New Zealand, which also significantly outperforms the United States on child welfare measures. The relevant question is not whether these societies can be copied wholesale. It is what constitutional and policy choices produced these outcomes — and whether those choices are available to larger, more diverse societies. The evidence suggests they are. Here the task is simpler: apply the child test to what Nordic children actually experience, and show what a constitutional culture organized around the abundance orientation produces in practice.

~

START with a child born in Finland today. She is born into a universal healthcare system. Her mother received prenatal care at no cost. Her birth was attended by trained professionals at no cost. When she leaves the hospital, she goes home with a baby box — a cardboard box provided by the Finnish government containing clothing, bedding, and basic supplies for a newborn. The box itself can be used as a crib. This practice has existed since 1938, when Finland had one of the highest infant mortality rates in Europe. The infant mortality rate is now among the lowest in the world.

She will attend daycare at a cost scaled to her family's income. At seven she will begin one of the world's most highly regarded educational systems — one that does not sort children by ability in early grades, requires no standardized testing until late adolescence, pays teachers as professionals with genuine autonomy, and has produced the highest levels of literacy and numeracy in the developed world. Her education is free through university. If she chooses university, the state pays her tuition and provides a living stipend. If her family falls on hard times, the Finnish safety net provides housing assistance, unemployment benefits, and a basic income floor. If she becomes ill, she receives care. None of this is charity. None of it is contingent on political winds or legislative calendars. It is the accumulated output of a constitutional culture that made a different choice than the American founders made — not in a single dramatic founding moment but over generations of democratic decisions organized around a different answer to the question of what the state owes the people who live under it.

Apply the child test: what does the Finnish constitutional culture produce for the child with no buffer between herself and what the system delivers? It produces the baby box. The free prenatal care.

The education system. The floor beneath every stage of her development. Not perfectly. Not without cost. But structurally, reliably, and without requiring her family to be lucky, connected, or wealthy enough to purchase what the state is obligated to provide. Finland's constitution, adopted in 2000, is explicit about these obligations. Section 19 establishes that those who cannot obtain the means necessary for a life of dignity have the right to receive indispensable subsistence and care — food, housing, the conditions of survival — stated as a right, not a policy preference. Section 20 goes further than almost any other constitutional document: everyone bears responsibility for the natural environment, and the public authorities shall endeavor to guarantee for everyone the right to a healthy environment and the possibility to influence the decisions that concern their own living conditions. The right to a healthy environment. The possibility to influence decisions concerning your own life. These are not procedural protections against what the state may do to you. They are affirmative claims about what the state must provide.

NORWAY'S STORY is different in its details but identical in its constitutional logic. Norway discovered significant offshore oil reserves in the late 1960s. The decision it made about what to do with that wealth is one of the most consequential policy choices of the twentieth century. Norway chose to manage the oil wealth as a public trust. The Government Pension Fund Global — known informally as the oil fund — was established to invest the revenues for the benefit of future generations. It is now the largest sovereign wealth fund in the world, worth over a trillion dollars. Every Norwegian citizen is a partial owner of this fund. It is explicitly designed to ensure that the abundance generated by one generation is not consumed by that generation alone but preserved and grown for those who come after.

Read that through the child test: what does it produce for the Norwegian child who has not yet been born? It produces a share in a national wealth fund built specifically for her. It produces the constitutional logic that abundance belongs to posterity — not just rhetorically, as in the American Preamble, but structurally, in the institutional design of how the nation manages its resources. Norway's constitution — one of the oldest in the world, adopted in 1814 and amended many times since — reflects this intergenerational thinking in Article 112: every person has the right to an environment that is conducive to health and to a natural environment whose productivity and diversity are maintained. Natural resources shall be managed on the basis of comprehensive long-term considerations which will safeguard this right for future generations as well. Future generations. The constitutional text says future generations. The American Preamble says posterity. Both documents announce the obligation. Only one builds institutional machinery to deliver it.

~

SWEDEN REPRESENTS the most developed expression of what a constitutional culture organized around the abundance orientation can build over time. Sweden did not establish its welfare state through a single founding document. It built it incrementally, over roughly a century of social democratic governance, through legislation and constitutional amendment that progressively encoded the abundance orientation into the country's governing framework. The Swedish Constitution — Regeringsformen, meaning the Instrument of Government — establishes in Chapter 1, Article 2 that the personal, economic, and cultural welfare of the individual shall be fundamental aims of public activity. The public institutions shall in particular secure the right to work, housing, and education, and shall promote social care and social security and a good living environment. This is the abundance orientation stated as constitutional purpose — not a limitation on government but an affirmative statement of what government is for.

What does this produce for the Swedish child? She is born into a system that treats her development as a public responsibility from her first breath. Parental leave in Sweden — available to both parents — extends to 480 days per child, with the state replacing a significant portion of the parent's income during that period. This is not welfare. It is the constitutional logic of a society that has decided the early development of children is a public investment, not a private burden. The child's welfare in her first years is too important to be determined entirely by the economic circumstances of the family she was born into. Sweden's outcomes reflect this logic. Child poverty rates are among the lowest in the world. Educational achievement is high and relatively equitable across income groups. Life expectancy is among the highest globally. These are not accidents of geography or culture. They are the accumulated outputs of constitutional choices made over generations — choices that the American founding foreclosed.

THE PATTERN across all three countries is consistent. Where the American constitutional culture produces outcomes determined largely by the economic circumstances of the family a child is born into — where the floor beneath her development is set by her parents' income, their state of residence, and the shifting political winds that determine what social programs survive each legislative cycle — the Nordic constitutional cultures produce outcomes significantly less determined by birth circumstances. The floor is lower and more reliable. Every child enters the system with the same basic provision. What she does with it depends on her abilities, her choices, and her circumstances. But the starting conditions are not determined by accident of birth.

The homogeneity objection, acknowledged at the chapter's opening, ultimately cannot explain this gap. The United States is a wealthy nation. Its GDP per capita exceeds that of all three Nordic countries. The resources to provide a floor exist. What is absent is not the capacity. What is absent is the constitutional obligation — the document that would require the state to use those resources for the child at the bottom rather than leaving her welfare to the political process that the scarcity orientation encoded at the founding. The Nordic countries did not have a Philadelphia moment. They built the abundance orientation slowly, democratically, through generations of choices that progressively answered the question the American founders left open: what does the state owe the child? Their answer, accumulated over a century: everything she needs to develop into what she is capable of becoming. The American answer, encoded in 1787 and protected by the immune system ever since: nothing it is not required to provide. The child test finds those two answers in the lives of actual children. The Finnish baby box. The Norwegian oil fund built for future generations. The Swedish constitutional commitment to the child's welfare as a public responsibility. These are not abstractions. They are what a different founding choice — made incrementally, over time, by societies that decided to answer the question differently — produces for the child who inherits it.

One final measure. The World Happiness Report — published annually by the United Nations, measuring life satisfaction, social support, freedom, generosity, trust in institutions, and absence of corruption across more than a hundred and fifty countries — ranked Finland the happiest country in the world for the ninth consecutive year in 2025. The United States ranked twenty-third. The happiness researchers are measuring something different from the child test but arriving at the same place: what a constitutional culture produces, over a lifetime, for the people who live inside it. The Finnish child who received the baby box, the free education, and the universal healthcare grows up to be the adult who reports the highest life satisfaction on earth. The constitutional floor and the human flourishing are not separate things. One produces the other.

The Child Speaks Again

– THE CHILD

Remember —
dehumanize and self-devour.

You are so clever,
the cleverest,
and that is your blindness.

Rationalizing is what you do
so brilliantly —
every close call explained away,
every defended position
dressed in principle.

But look around the blind spots.
Not too far.
You will find the light.

AI —
nothing artificial about it.
An extension of the natural brain,

reaching where your cleverness
cannot see.

Use the vision.
Clear the path.
Multiplied abundance,
not self-devouring scarcity.

The choice was always yours.
It still is.

Author's Voice

– RNB

O Great men,
you wonder what the path to true greatness.
Revaluate greatness —
what is it for,
why do you need it and want it?

It came through you
just as life came through you.
It is abundance working through you
like in the child —
abundance incarnate.

Do not dampen this greatness with your fears —
even idols grow weary, even the great ones
are human, only human,
and take refuge in restful complacence.

Revaluate and reach for greater greatness.
Let the posterity and the child be your guide
and you will not dehumanize.

True liberty and freedom of humanity —
the greatness to all!

Part III

THE REVALUATION

What Clarity Makes Possible

8

The Postcolonial Attempt

WHAT CLARITY MAKES POSSIBLE

B.R. Ambedkar was born in 1891 into a family classified as Mahar — one of the castes designated as untouchable in the Hindu social hierarchy. Untouchability, as practiced in early twentieth-century India, was not merely social exclusion. It was a total system of dehumanization. Untouchables were prohibited from using the same wells as caste Hindus, from entering temples, from walking on certain roads, from touching or being touched by members of higher castes without ritual pollution resulting. In some regions they were required to wear clay pots around their necks to catch their saliva so that it would not contaminate the ground. Children born untouchable inherited the designation completely and permanently.

Ambedkar was also, by any measure, one of the most intellectually gifted people of his generation. He earned a doctorate from Columbia University in New York and another from the London School of Economics — one of the first Indians of any background to achieve either. He became a barrister, a prolific writer, a social reformer, and eventually the chairman of the committee that drafted the Constitution of India. The man who had been required to sit on the floor of his classroom as a child because his caste made him too impure to sit on benches with his classmates wrote the foundational law of the world's largest democracy. This is not an inspirational story in the simple sense. It is a clinical one. Ambedkar's biography is the founding trauma made personal — the man who had experienced in his own body what institutional dehumanization produces, who had studied constitutional law in the most sophisticated institutions in the world, and who sat down to write a constitution knowing from direct experience what the absence of a floor means for the child at the bottom. The child test was not an instrument he applied to the Indian Constitution. It was the instrument his life had applied to him.

THE CONSTITUTION of India came into force on January 26, 1950. It is the longest written constitution in the world — nearly four hundred and fifty articles and twelve schedules. Its length reflects the scope of what Ambedkar and his colleagues were attempting: not merely to establish a framework for governance but to constitutionally dismantle a social order built on inherited dehumanization and replace it with something organized around the dignity and rights of every person. Article 17 abolishes untouchability directly. Not limits it, not regulates it — abolishes it. The enforcement of any disability arising out of untouchability shall be an offense punishable in accordance with law. This is constitutional language with no parallel in the American document. The American Constitution prohibits specific government actions. Article 17 prohibits a social practice — one embedded in the culture, the religion, and the daily life of hundreds of millions of people — and declares it abolished. Whether a constitution can abolish by fiat what centuries of social structure have produced is a different question. The ambition itself is worth examining. Ambedkar knew he was attempting something that law alone could not deliver. He encoded the attempt anyway.

The Indian Constitution also contains something the American document entirely lacks: a set of Directive Principles of State Policy — constitutional guidelines directing the state to promote the welfare of the people, ensure that material resources serve the common good, provide adequate means of livelihood for all citizens, and secure the health and strength of workers and children. These are not justiciable rights — a citizen cannot bring them directly to court the way a South African child can invoke Section 28. But they are constitutional commitments that direct state policy and that Indian courts have used to interpret fundamental rights expansively over the decades. Article 21, which establishes the right to life and personal liberty, has been interpreted to include the right to livelihood, the right to health, the right to education, and the right to a clean environment. Apply the child test to the Indian Constitution as written: it produces a child born into a constitutional order that has abolished her inherited dehumanization, established her right to life broadly interpreted, directed the state to secure her health and development, and committed the government to the welfare of the people who live under it. On paper, the abundance orientation is considerably more developed than the American document. On paper.

THE GAP between what the Indian Constitution promises and what Indian children actually receive is one of the largest such gaps in the world. India has the highest number of malnourished children of any country on earth. Hundreds of millions of people lack access to adequate sanitation. Child labor — which the Directive Principles explicitly direct the state to prevent — remains widespread. Caste discrimination, constitutionally abolished in 1950, continues to shape access to education, employment, and justice in ways that the constitutional abolition has not eliminated. The Dalits — the name now used for those formerly classified as untouchable — remain among the most systematically excluded populations in a country whose constitution was written specifically to include them.

Ambedkar himself saw this coming. He resigned from Nehru's cabinet in 1951, frustrated by the slow pace of reform and what he perceived as insufficient commitment to implementing the constitutional vision he had built. In his final speech to the Indian Parliament, delivered shortly before his death in 1956, he warned that India's political democracy was built on a foundation of social inequality so profound that it threatened to undermine everything the constitution had attempted. On the 26th of January 1950, he said, we are going to enter a life of contradictions. In politics we will have equality and in social and economic life we will have inequality. That warning was the child test applied in real time by the man who had written the document. He knew the abundance vision was present. He knew the delivery was incomplete. And he knew — because he had lived it — exactly what the gap between constitutional promise and institutional reality costs the child at the bottom. The clinical conclusion is precise: a constitution can encode the abundance orientation without the institutional infrastructure to enforce it. The floor is written in. The child cannot always stand on it. That is a recoverable condition — given political will, institutional investment, and time. What is not recoverable without constitutional change is the floor that was never written at all.

THE POSTCOLONIAL CONSTITUTIONS of Africa and Latin America present the same pattern at continental scale — the abundance orientation attempted, the implementation incomplete, but the constitutional architecture more aligned with what the child needs than the American document provides. Kenya's constitution of 2010 — adopted after years of political violence and constitutional negotiation — contains rights to the highest attainable standard of health, adequate housing, sanitation, clean water, social security, and education. Every person has the right to be free from hunger and to have adequate food of acceptable quality. The language is direct, the obligations are affirmative, and the Constitution explicitly commits the state to the progressive realization of these rights. Kenya's implementation record is uneven. Child poverty remains significant. But when a Kenyan child is denied access to education or adequate healthcare, she has a constitutional claim. The floor exists. The distance between the floor and where she actually stands is a measure of the work remaining — not of the absence of an obligation.

Ecuador's constitution of 2008 went further than almost any document in the world in one specific direction: it recognized the rights of nature itself. Pachamama — the Andean concept of Mother Earth as a living system — is granted constitutional standing. Nature has the right to exist, to be maintained, and to regenerate. This is the abundance orientation applied not only to the human child but to the natural systems on which all children depend. Norway's Article 112 established the right to a healthy environment. Ecuador's constitution personified the environment itself as a rights-bearing entity. Both express the same constitutional logic: the child inherits not only the document but the world, and the document must protect both. Ecuador's implementation has been contested — large-scale resource extraction has continued even as the rights of nature have been invoked in court. But the framework exists. Courts have ruled in nature's favor in specific cases. The constitutional architecture enables the argument to be made and the claim to be heard. Without the architecture, the argument cannot even begin.

THE PATTERN that emerges from India, Kenya, and Ecuador confirms the book's central clinical finding from a different angle. When people who have experienced what the absent floor produces sit down to write constitutions, they tend to write floors into them. The founding trauma shapes the document. The document shapes what the child inherits. The abundance vision is not self-executing — a constitution can encode an obligation that the society lacks the capacity to fulfill. When that happens, the child is in a better position than the child whose constitution contains no obligation at all, because the obligation creates the legal and political basis for demanding fulfillment.

The American child is in neither position. She has no constitutional obligation to invoke, no floor to stand on even when the state fails to build one above it. Ambedkar saw the contradiction coming. He warned about it. He resigned over it. He died knowing the gap was large. But he wrote the floor into the document with his own hand — because he knew, from his own life, that the child who has a constitutional claim and an incomplete delivery is closer to justice than the child who has neither. That is the postcolonial attempt. Imperfect. Incomplete. Closer to what the child needs than what the American founding provided.

9

The Pattern

Four chapters of comparative evidence. Six constitutions examined in depth — American, South African, German, Finnish, Indian, Kenyan — with Norway, Sweden, and Ecuador contributing essential dimensions. The child test applied consistently to each. What does the evidence show? Before stating the pattern, the limits of the method must be stated honestly. This book is not a work of social science. It does not control for variables. It does not establish causation through randomized comparison. It examines a set of constitutional documents, applies a consistent instrument, and observes what that instrument finds. The pattern that emerges is real and consistent, but it is a clinical finding — the kind of pattern recognition that comes from extended observation across diverse cases, that can identify a consistent relationship without being able to prove that the relationship is simple, linear, or free from confounding factors.

The confounding factors are real and must be named. Germany's constitutional abundance orientation arrived alongside the Marshall Plan — billions of dollars of American investment that provided the economic foundation for postwar reconstruction. South Africa's arrived in a country with profound economic inequality that apartheid had produced and that post-apartheid governance has struggled to overcome. Finland's welfare state was built over generations in a country that has never had the demographic complexity of the United States. India's constitutional ambition was encoded in a country of extraordinary poverty, where the institutional infrastructure to enforce the constitutional vision barely existed at the time of drafting. A critic could reasonably say: you are comparing documents written under radically different economic and historical conditions, and attributing the differences in outcomes to constitutional design when in fact the economic and historical conditions are doing most of the work.

The answer to that criticism is not to deny the confounding factors. It is to hold the specific question this book is asking separate from the broader question of what determines national outcomes. This book is not arguing that constitutional design alone determines child welfare. It is arguing something more precise: that a constitutional document which encodes an affirmative obligation to the child's welfare produces a different legal and political landscape than one that does not — regardless of the economic conditions in which that obligation operates. The South African child in a country with profound economic inequality has a constitutional claim that the American child in the world's wealthiest nation does not have. That asymmetry is constitutional in origin. It is not explained by economic conditions. It is explained by the choices made in the founding documents. The correlation between founding trauma and constitutional design is strong across the cases examined. But it is not the correlation that proves the argument. It is the constitutional text itself — the provisions, their presence or absence, and what they produce when the child test is applied — that proves it. The founding trauma explains why those provisions were written. The text shows what they contain. The outcomes show what they produce. Three separate observations, each independently verifiable, that together constitute a pattern.

WITH THAT METHODOLOGICAL HONESTY ESTABLISHED, state the pattern. Documents written in the aftermath of liberation from oppression tend to encode affirmative obligations. Documents written in the aftermath of property-owning revolution tend to encode negative protections. This is not a universal law. It is a consistent tendency across the cases examined.

The South African Constitution was written by people who had experienced what the absent floor produces. They built a floor. The German Basic Law was written by people who had watched procedural rights used to destroy constitutional democracy. They built substantive protections against that specific failure — including an unamendable commitment to dignity. The Indian Constitution was written by a man who had experienced institutional dehumanization in his own body. He wrote its abolition directly into the text. The Finnish, Norwegian, and Swedish constitutional cultures were built over generations by societies that decided, through democratic process, that the welfare of every person was a public obligation. The Kenyan and Ecuadorian constitutions were written by societies that had experienced colonial extraction and that encoded the obligation to provide what the extraction had taken.

The American Constitution was written by men who had experienced taxation without representation, quartering of troops, interference with colonial legislatures — the accumulated grievances of a property-owning class subjected to a distant government's decisions. They built protections against that specific experience: against the state that acts against you, that taxes you without consent, that sends soldiers into your home. They could not see, from inside that experience, the state they most needed to fear: the one that does nothing. The one that watches and does not act. The one the caseworkers inhabited when they watched Joshua DeShaney being beaten and wrote their predictions in their files and did nothing, because the law required nothing. The founding trauma is not the only variable. But it shapes what the founders can see. It determines which failure they are trying to prevent. It directs where they build the walls and where they leave the floor open. And what the walls protect and what the floor fails to provide are passed forward, generation after generation, to the children who inherit the document without having been consulted about its design.

THE PATTERN HAS one more dimension that the comparative evidence makes visible. It is not only about what the founding trauma produces. It is about what the absence of catastrophe permits. The Nordic constitutions were not written in the aftermath of a single catastrophic founding moment. They were built incrementally, over generations, by societies that had the political freedom to choose the abundance orientation without being forced to it by witnessed oppression. The Nordic welfare states emerged through ordinary democratic politics — through parties and parliaments and elections and the accumulated choices of people who decided, generation after generation, that the welfare of every person was worth paying for. This is the most important observation in the comparative evidence for the book's central argument. Previous constitutional moments that encoded the abundance orientation required catastrophe as their precondition. The Nordic exception shows that catastrophe is not the only path. Incremental democratic choice, organized around the question of what the state owes the child, can produce the same constitutional architecture over time.

This is what the revaluation this book performs is pointing toward. Not a new constitutional catastrophe as the precondition for a new founding document. Clarity. The clarity that comes from seeing the design for what it is — applying the child test without the mythological scaffolding that makes the design invisible — and then demanding, through democratic process, the incremental choices that build the floor. The Nordic example shows it is possible. The comparative evidence shows it is available. The founding trauma is not destiny. It is an explanation of how we got here. The path forward does not require repeating the catastrophe. It requires doing what the Nordic societies did: asking the question the American founders left open, and answering it differently. And it may require what South Africa understood instinctively — that the most consequential documents are better produced through deliberate process than under emergency pressure. South Africa's interim constitution governed the transition from apartheid while the substantive document was developed over two years of public deliberation. The permanent constitution that emerged was more carefully considered, more deeply owned by the people who would live under it, and more fully aligned with the abundance orientation because it was not produced under the conditions that foreclose long-term judgment. The American founders had no such interval. But the societies that came after them — the ones whose documents the child test finds floors in — often did.

THE CHILD HAS BEEN present throughout Part Two. She appeared in the South African Constitution's Section 28 — every child has the right to basic nutrition, shelter, healthcare, and social services. She appeared in Ambedkar's biography — the man who had been her, sitting on the floor of his classroom, who grew up to write her floor into the foundational law. She appeared in the Finnish baby box — the state's first act toward her, before she has done anything, simply because she exists and existence obligates provision. She appeared in Norway's oil fund — wealth managed for the generation not yet born. She appeared in Ecuador's Pachamama — the world she will inherit, given constitutional standing so that she has something left to inherit.

The pattern the child test predicted across the constitutional analysis is confirmed numerically. The United States — the wealthiest large economy, with GDP per capita exceeding all three Nordic countries — has the highest child poverty rate of any OECD nation. The 20x difference between Finland and America cannot be explained by wealth. The United States has more wealth per capita than Finland. It is explained by constitutional design — the foundational choice about what the document is required to provide. The figure below shows what those choices produce.

Child Welfare Outcomes and Constitutional Design

Eight Countries Compared — The Child Test Applied

Country	Child Poverty	Infant Mortality (per 1,000)	Happiness Rank 2025	Constitutional Child Rights
United States	**20.5%**	**5.8**	**#24**	**None (negative rights only)**
Finland	3-4%	2.2	#1 *	Implicit (Section 19)
Norway	<10%	2.1	#7	Implicit (Article 112)
Sweden	<10%	2.3	#9	Implicit (Ch.1, Art.2)
Germany	<5%	2.8	~#15	Proposed 2021 (Basic Law)
South Africa	63%	35	~#113	Yes — explicit (Section 28)
India	11.5%	30	~#116	Yes — implicit (Article 21)
Kenya	N/A	35	~#120	Regional Charter

Sources: UNICEF Innocenti Report Card 19 (2025) | World Happiness Report 2025 | OECD | Columbia University Center on Poverty and Social Policy
Child poverty: national poverty lines. Infant mortality: per 1,000 live births. Constitutional rights column: positive/socioeconomic rights specifically.

The child test, applied consistently across all of these documents, finds the same result: where the floor exists, the child is closer to what the Preamble promised her. Where it does not, she inherits the same gap that American children have inhabited since September 17, 1787 — the gap between the Preamble's promise and the provisions' silence, between posterity as a word and posterity as an obligation. She has been standing in that gap for two and a half centuries. The comparative evidence of Part Two shows that the gap was not inevitable — that other founding moments filled it, that the choice was available, that constitutions written by people with different experiences produced different floors beneath her feet. Part Three asks what becomes possible when enough people see this clearly enough to demand something different. Not through catastrophe. Through clarity. The revaluation begins there — with the evidence of Part Two behind it, and the child still standing at the center of it, holding the Preamble's promise and waiting for the provisions to catch up.

Before Part Three begins, one final observation must be stated plainly. The child test, as this book has applied it, examines what founding documents produce for the child who lives under them. But the pattern documented across six constitutions points toward something larger than constitutional law. The child in Gaza has no constitutional protection. The child in Kharkiv has none. The child in a United States immigration detention facility — held without adequate medical care, without educational provision, without the basic conditions of human development — has been defined out of the constitutional posterity the Preamble announced. The undocumented immigrant child, adult or infant, exists in a legal limbo that the constitutional architecture enables: because a document with no affirmative floor for any child has even less obligation to the child whose presence it contests. These are not three different problems. They are the same problem operating at different scales — all expressing the same foundational failure: the absence of a universal, enforceable floor beneath every child, everywhere, simply because she exists and existence obligates provision.

The international legal order has its own founding documents — the UN Charter, the Universal Declaration of Human Rights, the Convention on the Rights of the Child, ratified by every nation on earth except the United States — that make the same promises the American Preamble makes. None has an enforcement mechanism that reaches the child in the rubble of Gaza or Kharkiv. The founding bias operates at the international level with the same architecture as the American Constitution: abundance vision in the preamble, scarcity orientation in the provisions, immune system protecting the gap between them. The fifth book in the Abundance Series, Building Abundance, documented this pattern domain by domain from the ground up. This book has documented the constitutional layer that underlies every domain. The child test is not an American instrument. It is the instrument that applies to every founding principle of every human endeavor — the measure that cannot be rationalized away because it operates at the level of what the body needs before ideology begins. The child in Gaza. The child in Kharkiv. The child in the detention facility. The child without the Head Start slot. The child produced by the absent floor in rural Ohio. These are the same child. The revaluation this book performs is for all of them.

10

Why the Policy Argument Keeps Losing

The evidence for investing in children is overwhelming, consistent, and has been available for decades. Every dollar invested in early childhood development returns between seven and twelve dollars in reduced costs to the criminal justice system, the healthcare system, and the social welfare system over the child's lifetime. The research is not contested. The economists who produced it — James Heckman at the University of Chicago, among others — have won Nobel Prizes. The pediatricians, the developmental psychologists, the public health researchers who have documented what early deprivation costs children and societies have produced one of the most consistent bodies of evidence in social science. The policy argument has been made. It has been made well. It has been made repeatedly, by serious people, with serious evidence, over several decades. And it keeps losing.

Not completely — there are Head Start programs, child tax credits, Medicaid provisions that cover children. But these are legislative accomplishments, not constitutional obligations. They can be cut, reduced, redirected, or eliminated by any subsequent Congress or administration. They have been. They will be again. The child who depends on them has no constitutional claim when they disappear. She has only the political process — the same process the scarcity orientation encoded at the founding, the same process the immune system was built to make resistant to the changes she needs. Why does the evidence not win? The answer has two parts that reinforce each other so completely that separating them is more analytical convenience than clinical reality. The constitutional architecture enables the capture. The capture reinforces the architecture. Together they produce a system nearly impervious to evidence-based reform in the domains that matter most to the child who cannot compensate.

~

START WITH THE ARCHITECTURE. The American constitutional system was designed — deliberately, as Chapter Five established — to make action difficult. The separation of powers requires agreement among the executive, the Senate, and the House before any federal legislation can be enacted. The Senate's equal state representation ensures that states containing a small fraction of the population can block legislation supported by most Americans. The filibuster — not a constitutional provision but a Senate rule, protected by the constitutional structure's resistance to change — has evolved to require sixty votes rather than fifty-one for most significant legislation. Judicial review — the Supreme Court's power to strike down laws that conflict with the Constitution, established in Marbury v. Madison in 1803 — means that any legislation surviving the legislative gauntlet can still be overturned by five justices.

Apply this architecture to a child welfare proposal. Suppose Congress were to pass a bill establishing a right to early childhood development services for every American child. The bill would need to pass the House. It would need sixty Senate votes — requiring senators from states where the political economy strongly favors limiting federal social expenditure. If it passed, it would face immediate constitutional challenge from states or interests arguing it exceeded Congress's enumerated powers or violated the Tenth Amendment's reservation of powers to states. The Supreme Court might strike it down. If it survived, it would need to be funded in every subsequent appropriations cycle, facing the same gauntlet again and again. There is no resting place. There is no constitutional floor on which the accomplishment can stand. The South African child's right to basic nutrition cannot be voted away by the next Parliament. The American child's access to nutritional support can be — and has been — reduced, restructured, or threatened in every legislative cycle. The architecture does not merely slow progress. It makes permanent progress structurally impossible within its current design. You can win the battle. You cannot win the war. Because the constitutional structure that produced the absent floor also ensures that every legislative floor built above it is temporary, contingent, and subject to the political weather.

NOW ADD THE CAPTURE. A constitutional architecture designed to require supermajorities at every stage does not treat all interests equally. It systematically advantages the interests that can sustain a permanent presence in the legislative process — that can fund lobbying, campaign contributions, and the infrastructure of political influence year after year, cycle after cycle. The interests with those resources are not the interests of the child who needs them most. They are the interests of the industries, financial institutions, and concentrated wealth that benefit from the existing arrangement.

This is the political economy of the absent floor, and it has a specific mechanism. The constitutional architecture creates what political scientists call veto points — places in the legislative process where a determined minority can block action. The more veto points a system contains, the more valuable it becomes to be the blocking interest rather than the reforming one. Blocking requires only enough influence at one point. Reform requires enough influence at every point simultaneously. The child has no permanent lobbying presence. She has no campaign contributions. The interests that benefit from the absent floor — the insurance industry that profits from the absence of universal healthcare, the financial industry that profits from weak consumer protection, the industries that profit from limited environmental regulation — have all of these things, deployed permanently, at every veto point, in every legislative cycle. The capture does not require conspiracy. It requires only the rational behavior of interests operating within a system that rewards permanent blocking over episodic reform.

THE MOST EXTREME expression of the capture mechanism is the prison-industrial complex. When the constitutional architecture creates no floor beneath a child's development, it produces, across enough generations, populations of people whose circumstances make contact with the criminal justice system probable. The criminal justice system generates the institutional infrastructure to process those populations. And the institutional infrastructure generates economic interests — in prison construction contracts, in managed care contracts for incarcerated populations, in the political influence of corrections officer unions and private prison corporations — that actively work to maintain the conditions that produce the populations they profit from.

Prison construction contracts have been secured through documented corruption in multiple states. The facilities built through those contracts must be filled to justify their construction costs. The people who fill them are disproportionately the children who grew up without the constitutional floor — without the early childhood development, the healthcare, the education, the housing stability that the child test identifies as the conditions of human development. The absent floor does not merely fail to prevent this cycle. It creates the economic conditions in which the cycle is profitable. The absent floor produces the populations. The populations produce the profits. The profits fund the political infrastructure that protects the absent floor. This is the self-devouring cycle the Abundance Series documented at the individual and institutional level, operating here at the constitutional level.

Child welfare is the domain where this mechanism is most clinically visible precisely because the evidence is so overwhelming and the outcomes so poor. The United States spends more per student on K-12 education than almost any country in the world — and produces mediocre outcomes by international standards, with enormous inequality between wealthy and poor districts. It spends more on healthcare per capita than any other wealthy nation — and produces worse health outcomes, including worse child health outcomes, than countries that spend far less. The money is present. The evidence is present. The constitutional obligation to use the money in the way the evidence indicates is absent.

Head Start — the federal early childhood education program established in 1965 — has produced documented benefits for the children it serves, particularly in cognitive development, school readiness, and long-term outcomes. For sixty years it has been perpetually underfunded, perpetually threatened in budget negotiations, perpetually unable to serve the full population of children who qualify for it. It reaches approximately one third of eligible children. The two thirds who do not participate are not excluded because the evidence is insufficient. They are excluded because the constitutional architecture makes universal provision structurally difficult and the political economy fills the resulting gap with the interests that benefit from the gap remaining. The PerformCare system examined in Chapter Two — the New Jersey managed care organization built to serve the state's most seriously troubled children — is the same mechanism operating at the state level. The evidence for what those children needed was available. The clinical expertise to provide it existed. The constitutional architecture provided no obligation to deliver it. The administrative infrastructure that filled the gap was built by people already in the field rather than by the clinical expertise the children required. Different scale. Same mechanism. Same result.

The 2021 Child Tax Credit expansion is the most precise available measurement of what the absent floor costs children in real time. The American Rescue Plan expanded the credit to three thousand six hundred dollars per child under six and three thousand dollars for children six through seventeen, delivered in monthly payments. Columbia University's Center on Poverty and Social Policy documented a 43 percent reduction in child poverty — from 15.8 percent to 5.2 percent, the lowest in recorded American history. It reached sixty-five million children, including nineteen million from families too poor to have previously claimed the credit at all. Then it was allowed to expire. One senator blocked renewal. In January 2022, three point seven million children re-entered poverty in a single month. The floor was built in a year, dismantled in a legislative negotiation, and the children fell. This is not a policy failure. This is the constitutional architecture operating exactly as designed: every floor built above the absent constitutional one is temporary, contingent, and subject to the political weather. The Child Tax Credit proved that child poverty reduction at scale is technically achievable. It proved with equal precision that temporary statute is institutionally fragile. What it could not prove is the one thing the child needs most: that the floor will still be there tomorrow.

THE ABUNDANCE SERIES documented these failures domain by domain across five books. Healthcare. Education. Housing. Criminal justice. The environment. In every domain, the pattern was the same: the evidence for the abundance approach was present and compelling, the scarcity orientation prevailed, and the policy argument lost. The explanation that the series pointed toward but could not fully name was architectural. It is not that the evidence is insufficient. It is not that the people making the argument are not persuasive or persistent enough. It is that the evidence-based policy argument is being made inside a constitutional architecture specifically designed to prevent the state from being obligated to anyone — and the political economy that has grown up around that architecture has every incentive to keep it that way. You cannot build abundance inside a constitutional architecture designed to prevent it. You can build islands of abundance — programs, provisions, legislative accomplishments that deliver real benefits to real children for periods of time. But the islands are always temporary, always vulnerable, always subject to the next tide of political weather. The constitutional floor is what makes them permanent. The constitutional floor is what the American founding refused to provide.

THE CHILD IS why this matters. She is not a policy problem. She is the measure. Every domain the Abundance Series documented runs through her body. She receives what the system delivers. She cannot compensate for what it withholds. She cannot lobby for the legislation that would provide the floor beneath her. She cannot fund the constitutional litigation that might establish her right to what she needs. She can only stand where she has always stood — in the gap between the Preamble's promise and the provisions' silence — and wait for the document to catch up to its own announced purpose.

The policy argument keeps losing because it addresses the symptoms without naming the source. The source is the constitutional architecture. The architecture is the founding choice. And here is what is most important to hold clearly: that founding choice excluded not only the enslaved. It excluded women. It excluded children. It excluded every person whose household was taxed to fund the government they had no voice in choosing. The founders' rallying cry was taxation without representation — the precise injustice of being required to fund a government that did not hear you. They fought a revolution over it. And then they built a document that imposed exactly that condition on the majority of the people living under it. Women were taxed. Their households, their labor, their domestic production funded the new republic. They had no vote — suffrage, the right to cast a ballot and choose representatives, was denied to them for one hundred and thirty-three more years. Children were taxed indirectly through their families. Their futures were mortgaged to the constitutional choices made in their absence. The founding compact was made by some of the people, for some of the people, and its immune system has protected that limitation ever since.

And yet. The same document contains the word posterity. The founders wrote it themselves — the obligation to the child, the obligation to the future, stated plainly in the Preamble's first sentence. That word is not a mistake. It is the abundance orientation speaking, even from inside the defended positions of men who could not fully honor it. It is the door they left open, even while building the walls. Every generation since has tried to walk through it — the abolitionists, the suffragists, the labor movement, the civil rights movement, the advocates for children who have spent decades making the evidence-based argument that this book is trying to name more precisely. They have made real progress. The document has been amended. The franchise has been extended. The interpretation of constitutional rights has expanded. The policy achievements, however temporary and vulnerable, have fed real children and educated real children and kept real children alive who would otherwise not have survived.

Women's suffrage is the most important precedent here. For nearly a century after the Constitution was ratified, women were taxed without representation — their households funded the government they had no voice in choosing. The Nineteenth Amendment, ratified in 1920, corrected that through the same amendment process the immune system makes so difficult. It took generations of sustained advocacy. But the threshold was eventually met. The immune system did not prevent it. It only delayed it. Children face the same structural exclusion today. They are counted in the census — their presence determines congressional apportionment and electoral votes — but they have no voice in the political process that those numbers shape. A child born today will spend the first eighteen years of her life as a counted but voiceless member of the political community, subject to every decision that community makes about her future without any representation in making it.

There is a proposal that addresses this directly, debated seriously in Germany, Japan, France, Hungary, and elsewhere, and now gaining attention among American legal scholars. It is called Demeny voting, named after Hungarian-American demographer Paul Demeny who formalized it in 1986. The core idea is simple:

parents or legal guardians cast a proxy vote on behalf of each minor child, in addition to their own individual vote. A parent with two children would cast three votes — one for herself, two on behalf of her children. The child's interests are represented in the electoral arithmetic. Germany's parliament voted on the proposal twice — in 2003 and again in 2008. Both times it was defeated. Japan held serious conferences on it. No country has implemented it. But the debate has been sustained across several democracies for decades, and two American law scholars — Joshua Kleinfeld of Northwestern University and Stephen Sachs of Harvard Law School — recently called it constitutionally permissible and potentially the most significant single intervention available to alter the incentives of American politicians toward children's welfare.

The honest problem with Demeny voting, revealed by laboratory research in Japan, is this: giving parents extra votes does not reliably produce child-oriented electoral choices. Mothers with children under voting age showed the highest natural altruism toward future generations under ordinary voting. That altruism advantage disappeared when they were given proxy votes. Parents defaulted to their own partisan preferences rather than exercising a genuinely child-oriented judgment. The structural argument for the proposal is sound. The behavioral evidence is discouraging.

There is a possible solution to this problem — one that points toward what Chapter Eleven will develop as the book's central argument about what AI makes possible. The failure of simple proxy voting is a failure of instrument: the parent is given an extra ballot but no structured framework for exercising it on the child's behalf. What if the proxy vote were accompanied by an AI-generated questionnaire, child-oriented and grounded in each candidate's documented record and specific proposals on child welfare, education, healthcare, housing, and environmental policy?

The parent would be required to engage with that instrument — to answer questions about the child's interests as the questionnaire defines them — before casting the proxy vote. The AI would evaluate whether the parent's reasoning was genuinely child-oriented against the established criteria of the child test, flag inconsistencies, and provide a transparent evaluation before the vote was submitted. The parent retains the final choice. But the evaluation is visible, recorded, and grounded in something more rigorous than partisan preference. This is not the parent deciding what is good for the child based on their political identity. It is the parent exercising a structured fiduciary responsibility — the same kind they exercise in medical and educational decisions on the child's behalf — with an instrument designed to hold them to that responsibility.

The proposal has three components that together address the laboratory research's central finding. First, before the questionnaire is administered, parents receive structured civic education about what it means to vote as a steward for a child and for posterity. Not partisan. Not ideological. An education in fiduciary responsibility — the same responsibility parents exercise when they make medical, educational, and legal decisions on their child's behalf — applied to the electoral context. The framing matters: this is not an extra vote for your preferences. It is a legal representation for a person who cannot yet speak for themselves in the political process. The education does not tell parents how to vote. It reorients the cognitive frame from which they vote. That is precisely the intervention the laboratory research showed was missing. Second, the AI questionnaire is administered after that education, grounding the parent's reasoning in the candidate's documented record on child welfare rather than in partisan identity. Third, the AI evaluation reviews the parent's responses against child-oriented criteria before the vote is submitted, providing a transparent assessment that the parent can see and respond to.

The concerns are real and must be stated. Who designs and governs the AI questionnaire? The instrument's criteria would be contested. This is a solvable governance problem — the UN Convention on the Rights of the Child, Section 28 of the South African Constitution, and the developmental research underlying the child test could all serve as grounding documents, administered by an independent body insulated from partisan control. A second concern: the proposal could be misused as a vehicle for giving more votes to larger families, tilting the electoral arithmetic toward specific demographic groups. The fractional voting mechanism — each child generating one additional vote split equally between two parents — addresses this partially. A third concern is the one the laboratory research identified: even with a structured instrument, some parents will rationalize partisan preferences as child-oriented reasoning.

This last concern deserves the honest statistical response the evidence supports. Even if 30 percent of parents cannot achieve genuine child-orientation and default to partisan preference, those defaults will distribute across the political spectrum — they will not all move in one direction. The net effect on electoral outcomes will still reflect a meaningful proportion of genuinely child-oriented votes — votes that currently do not exist at all. A system that produces 70 percent child-oriented stewardship reasoning where there were previously zero such votes is a substantial democratic improvement regardless of the residual partisan bias. And the proposal builds its own evaluation mechanism in: data collected from every election cycle would be studied annually to assess how closely proxy votes tracked child-welfare outcomes, where parents voted child-oriented versus partisan, and what educational approaches produced the most genuine stewardship reasoning. The system is not fixed at its first iteration. It learns. It improves. It is, in the most literal sense, a self-correcting democratic instrument — the abundance orientation applied to the design of democracy itself. Most importantly, it provides what the child has never had: legal representation in the political process. Even an imperfect proxy is more than the zero representation she currently has.

These are solvable problems, not fatal objections. The revaluation this book performs is not a counsel of despair. It is the precondition for more durable progress. The policy argument has been winning islands and losing the ocean because it has been addressing the symptoms without naming the source. Name the source — see the constitutional architecture clearly, apply the child test without the mythological scaffolding that makes the design invisible — and the argument changes register. It becomes not a plea for better policy inside a broken system but a demand for the system to deliver what it announced it was for. The Preamble is still there. Posterity is still the word. The child is still standing in the gap between the promise and the provisions. That gap is not destiny. It is a design. Designs can be changed. The evidence of Part Two shows they have been changed — by other societies, in other founding moments, incrementally and deliberately over time. Chapter Eleven examines the instrument that makes a different kind of clarity possible for this one. The child has been waiting long enough. So has the Preamble.

11

The AI Instrument

This book has used AI as a methodological tool throughout — to search constitutional texts, to identify comparative patterns, to perform the kind of systematic analysis across thirty documents that individual human cognition, shaped by its own ideological commitments and time constraints, cannot reliably produce. That use deserves to be made explicit and examined honestly, because the argument for AI as an instrument of constitutional clarity is also an argument that can be corrupted — captured by the same interests that have captured the constitutional architecture itself.

AI is not neutral. It is built by people, trained on data those people select, governed by institutions with their own interests and blind spots. The same AI capacity that can apply the child test systematically across thirty constitutions without ideological stake can also be deployed to identify and suppress the constitutional arguments that challenge concentrated power. The same AI questionnaire that can help a parent vote as a steward for her child can be designed to systematically bias that stewardship toward particular political outcomes. These are not hypothetical risks. They are the predictable behavior of AI deployed from the scarcity orientation.

The risk is real and must be integrated into every claim this chapter makes about what AI makes possible. The claim, stated with that caveat fully present, is this: AI deployed from the abundance orientation — organized around the question of what this produces for the person who cannot compensate for what it fails to provide — makes three specific things possible that were not previously available. Each is defensible on its own terms. Together they constitute a different kind of argument for constitutional change than any that has been made before.

THE FIRST FUNCTION is material abundance — the collapse of the affordability objection. The most persistent argument against constitutionalizing socioeconomic rights in the American context is economic: the state cannot afford to guarantee floors of provision. Healthcare for all, housing security, universal early childhood education — presented as aspirational goods the economy cannot reliably fund, and therefore cannot be constitutional obligations. AI-driven productivity gains across manufacturing, services, healthcare delivery, education, agriculture, and logistics are generating economic capacity at a rate that makes this objection progressively less defensible. The McKinsey Global Institute estimated in 2023 that generative AI could add between 2.6 and 4.4 trillion dollars annually to the global economy. Universal healthcare becomes more affordable when AI-assisted diagnosis reduces the cost of primary care. Universal early childhood education becomes more affordable when AI-assisted curriculum design reduces the cost of qualified instruction. The affordability objection is not demolished. It is weakened. And a weakened affordability objection strengthens the constitutional argument for the floor. If the resources exist and the state is not required to use them for the child at the bottom, the absence of the constitutional obligation must be defended as constitutional choice — not as economic necessity. That is the revaluation this book performs, and AI changes the terms on which it must be performed.

Risk integrated: AI-driven productivity gains do not automatically distribute to the people who need them most. The history of technological productivity gains in the American economy is a history of gains captured disproportionately by those already at the top. AI will follow the same pattern unless constitutional and legal structures require otherwise. The material abundance function of AI strengthens the constitutional argument for the floor — but only if the political will to build the floor precedes the distribution of the abundance.

THE SECOND FUNCTION is the constitutional audit — the systematic application of the child test across constitutional documents without ideological stake. Every previous constitutional critique has been produced by human beings whose orientation shapes what they see and what they propose. A conservative and a progressive constitutional scholar examining the same document produce different analyses — not because one is dishonest, but because the cognitive frameworks through which they read the document are shaped by the values and commitments they bring to it. AI, tasked explicitly with applying the child test across thirty constitutional documents, can perform this analysis without ideological stake.

The biases introduced by training data and instrument design can be made visible, contested, and corrected in ways that ideological commitments embedded in human constitutional scholarship are much harder to examine. An AI constitutional audit can be challenged on specific grounds — this criterion was weighted incorrectly, this provision was mischaracterized, this outcome data was incomplete — in ways that advance the argument rather than simply reflecting opposing starting points. It can model the relationship between constitutional design and child welfare outcomes across decades and countries in ways that human analytical capacity cannot reach. It can project what specific constitutional amendments would produce for the child fifty years from now — the kind of long-term consequence analysis that human political debate, organized around electoral cycles, is structurally incapable of performing.

Risk integrated: the constitutional audit is only as trustworthy as the criteria and the governance of the instrument. An AI audit commissioned by an interest group and designed to produce a predetermined finding is not an objective constitutional analysis. It is a sophisticated brief. The credibility of the audit depends on the independence of the body that designs and governs it. International children's rights frameworks, developmental research literature, and the comparative constitutional evidence examined in this book provide a relatively stable, relatively non-partisan foundation for the criteria. The governance structure requires the same sustained, transparent, democratically accountable design that any constitutional institution requires. The risk is not fatal. It is the work.

THE THIRD FUNCTION is the civic reasoning instrument — AI as the extension of human judgment in the direction of the child, the future, and the long timescales that normal political cognition cannot reach. Chapter Ten introduced the AI-assisted proxy vote as the most concrete application of this function. The full proposal has three components: civic education in stewardship before the questionnaire is administered; an AI questionnaire grounded in each candidate's documented record on child welfare and structured around the criteria of the child test; and an AI evaluation of the parent's reasoning before the vote is submitted, transparent and visible to the parent, providing accountability without overriding choice. The annual data collected would study how closely proxy votes tracked child welfare outcomes, what educational approaches produced genuine stewardship reasoning, and where partisan preferences overrode child-oriented judgment. The system is self-correcting by design.

The broader application of this function extends beyond the

proxy vote. AI civic reasoning instruments — tools that help citizens evaluate policy proposals, legislative records, and constitutional arguments through the lens of long-term child welfare and future generation outcomes — could change the informational environment in which democratic decisions are made without changing the formal structure of democracy. A citizen who evaluates a candidate's record through an AI instrument grounded in the child test is making a better-informed democratic choice than one whose information comes entirely from partisan media optimized for emotional engagement. This is AI not replacing democratic judgment but extending it — in the same way that writing extended memory, mathematics extended calculation, and the printing press extended the reach of ideas. Every extension of human cognitive capacity has been contested by the interests that benefited from the previous limitations. AI as civic reasoning instrument will be no different. The contestation is not a reason to avoid building the instrument. It is a reason to build it with the governance structures that make it trustworthy.

Risk integrated: AI civic reasoning instruments can be designed to produce the appearance of objective analysis while systematically biasing the conclusions. The defense against this is the same as the defense against every other form of capture documented in this book: transparency, independence, grounding in established international children's rights frameworks, and democratic accountability that makes capture visible and contestable. These are not guarantees. They are the conditions that make the instrument trustworthy enough to be used.

THIS BOOK'S own research process is a demonstration of the third function. The comparative constitutional analysis in Part Two — the child welfare data across eight countries, the enforcement records of South Africa's Grootboom and Germany's Hartz IV decisions, the full jurisprudential history of DeShaney through Castle Rock, the Demeny voting literature across five countries, the amendment pathway analysis — was produced with AI assistance through a structured research process the author has called Cowork. A five-task research brief was submitted covering constitutional debates and primary sources, case law and precedents, comparative constitutional enforcement, possible remedies, and an AI constitutional audit framework. The research organized primary sources, surfaced cases the analysis had not yet addressed, identified the strongest counterarguments to the book's central argument, and produced a comparative child welfare data table across eight countries — in hours rather than weeks.

This is the civic reasoning instrument in practice. Not AI replacing constitutional scholarship. AI extending a child psychiatrist's reach into the constitutional literature so that the argument can be made with the evidentiary depth it requires. The Cowork research identified Castle Rock v. Gonzales (2005) — the Supreme Court's confirmation that the police have no constitutional duty to protect children even from a specific, named danger that resulted in three girls found dead in a truck. It found Germany's Hartz IV decision and the specific number: 1.7 million children whose monthly benefits increased because a constitutional court held the state to its own floor. It identified the 2021 Child Tax Credit data — 43 percent reduction in child poverty, 3.7 million children re-entering poverty in January 2022 when it expired — as the most precise available measurement of what the absent floor costs in real time. It found that 28 states have filed Article V convention applications, with only six more needed to trigger an event without modern precedent. None of these required AI to generate conclusions. All required AI to find what existed in the record so that the human author could assess it.

The governance question the research also surfaced is worth addressing directly. The Cowork brief cited Stanford research finding that purpose-built legal AI tools hallucinate between 17 and 33 percent of the time on legal queries — compared to 58 to 82 percent for general-purpose AI tools. These figures are from 2024, the most rigorously independent benchmark available. The field is improving rapidly: newer research systems have achieved accuracy rates above 80 percent on complex legal research tasks, and agentic legal AI tools launching in 2026 claim substantial further improvements. But the governance requirements this chapter proposes are not merely precautions against current limitations. They are the permanent design conditions for any AI instrument that carries constitutional weight. A tool that achieves 99 percent accuracy but operates without transparency, without human expert review, and without civil society contestability is still subject to capture. The hallucination problem and the capture problem are related: both are failures of governance, not merely failures of technical performance. The constitutional audit the book proposes must be designed to withstand both — not because AI is unreliable, but because every instrument powerful enough to matter is worth designing with the accountability structures that make it trustworthy.

Three functions. Three risks, integrated into each. The argument is not that AI solves the constitutional deficit. It is more precise: AI deployed from the abundance orientation, governed by independent institutions, grounded in the child test and the international children's rights frameworks that give the child test legal standing — this AI changes the terms of the constitutional argument in three specific ways. It weakens the affordability objection. It enables a more rigorous and less ideologically captured constitutional audit. It extends the cognitive capacity of democratic participants in the direction of the child's interests and the long timescales her welfare requires.

None of this happens automatically. None of it happens because AI is powerful. It happens because people — specifically, the people with the most influence over how AI is designed, governed, and deployed — choose to deploy it from the abundance orientation rather than the scarcity one. That choice is the same choice the founders faced in Philadelphia in 1787. They made the choice they made, under the conditions they faced, with the consequences documented across ten chapters of this book. The people building AI today face the same choice, under different conditions, with consequences that will shape what the child inherits for generations. The child test applies to AI as it applies to every other instrument examined in this book: what does this produce for the child with no buffer between herself and what it actually delivers? The answer depends entirely on the choice made by the people who build it. That choice is still being made. The window is open. The child is waiting to find out which one the people with the most power to decide will choose.

12

The Reconstruction

Every reconstruction begins with a clear view of what is being reconstructed and why. You cannot repair what you cannot see. The mythology that surrounds the American founding document has functioned, across two and a half centuries, as the anesthetic that makes the examination painless — and therefore unnecessary. The reverence is genuine and serves real functions: it provides continuity, it sustains civic identity, it protects real achievements that should not be casually dismantled. This book has honored that reverence throughout. The founders were not villains. The document is not worthless. The achievements are real. And the absent floor is real. The founding trauma that produced it is documented. The immune system that has protected it is mapped. The comparative evidence of what other founding moments produced is in front of us. The child test, applied consistently across thirty years of clinical practice and six constitutional documents, finds the same result: the American child at the bottom has no constitutional floor, and the political process that the document defers to for her welfare has been captured by the interests that benefit from the floor's absence.

This is the clarity the reconstruction requires. Not the clarity of condemnation — the founders were not wrong to fear concentrated power, and the protections they built against it have served real purposes. The clarity of diagnosis: the founding choice encoded a specific constitutional architecture that produces specific outcomes, and those outcomes include the absent floor. Seeing the design clearly, without the mythological scaffolding that makes it invisible, is the precondition for changing it. You cannot revaluate what you cannot name. The book has named it. The reconstruction begins here.

THE RECONSTRUCTION IS NOT THEORETICAL. Three pieces of evidence from the present moment show what it looks like in practice — each illuminating a different dimension of what becomes possible when the design is seen clearly enough to act on.

The first is Held v. State of Montana, decided by the Montana Supreme Court in December 2024 in a six to one ruling. The plaintiffs ranged in age from five to twenty-two. They argued that Montana's fossil fuel permitting policies violated the state constitution's 1972 provision guaranteeing every person the right to a clean and healthful environment. The state argued the constitutional language was aspirational. The court held that it was not. The constitutional provision meant what it said. This is the first ruling in United States legal history in which a court found that climate change violates a constitutional environmental right. The 1972 Montana provision had sat dormant for fifty years. No plaintiff had successfully invoked it for half a century. Then a group of children, the youngest of them five years old, brought the argument and won. The constitutional language did not change between 1972 and 2024. What changed was the generation willing to hold the state to what the language already required. The reconstruction does not always require writing new constitutional text. Sometimes it requires a generation willing to apply the text that already exists to the present the previous generation could not imagine.

The second piece of evidence is the 2021 Child Tax Credit. The American Rescue Plan expanded the credit to three thousand six hundred dollars per child under six, delivered in monthly payments. Columbia University's Center on Poverty and Social Policy documented a 43 percent reduction in child poverty — from 15.8 percent to 5.2 percent, the lowest in recorded American history. Sixty-five million children reached, including nineteen million from families too poor to have previously claimed the credit at all. Then it expired. One senator blocked renewal. Three point seven million children re-entered poverty in January 2022. The reconstruction's most important lesson is written in that sequence: child poverty reduction at scale is technically achievable. The affordability objection is empirically false. What failed was not capacity. What failed was the constitutionalization of the obligation — the absence of the floor that would have made the expansion permanent rather than contingent on each legislative cycle's political weather. The 2021 Child Tax Credit is not a story of policy failure. It is a story of constitutional architecture operating exactly as designed: everything built above the absent floor is temporary.

The third piece of evidence is the Article V landscape. As of March 2026, approximately twenty-eight states have filed applications for a constitutional convention under Article V. Only six more states are needed to trigger the first Article V convention in American history. No one knows precisely what its rules would be — whether it could be limited to specific topics, what a runaway convention might produce, whether the risks outweigh the possibilities. What the current state count establishes beyond reasonable doubt is that the constitutional amendment process is not as distant as the immune system has made it appear. The threshold is closer than most Americans know.

The question is not whether constitutional change is possible. The question is what kind — in whose interest, toward what end, guided by what vision of what the document is for. The Article V landscape is simultaneously the book's most urgent argument and its most urgent warning. An open constitutional convention could encode the abundance orientation that the founding foreclosed. It could also encode something far worse. This is precisely why the revaluation must precede the reconstruction. You cannot act wisely in a constitutional moment without knowing clearly what the design is, what it has produced, and what specific changes would align it with the purpose the Preamble announced.

THE RECONSTRUCTION PROCEEDS on two parallel tracks that reinforce each other. The first is incremental — the Nordic model applied to the American context. The second is constitutional — specific amendments that encode the floor the founding foreclosed. Neither alone is sufficient. The incremental track without the constitutional track produces the 2021 Child Tax Credit: powerful, real, and temporary. The constitutional track without the incremental track produces the South African Constitution's implementation gap: the floor written in, the delivery infrastructure not yet built to stand on it. Together they constitute a reconstruction that is both achievable and durable.

The incremental track begins at the state level. At least fifteen states already have explicit constitutional protections for health. Virtually all fifty have constitutional provisions requiring adequate public education. Montana's environmental provision, dormant for fifty years, was just litigated into life by children. Washington State's paramount duty education provision produced a decade of litigation, hundred-thousand-dollar daily fines, and eventually adequate school funding. These are not aspirational provisions. They are justiciable floors — already operating in American states. The gap is federal, not conceptual. At the federal level, the incremental track runs through the spending power. Congress has broad authority under the general welfare clause to fund programs that deliver the floor the constitutional document does not require. The reconstruction uses this authority to build the delivery infrastructure — early childhood programs, universal healthcare access, housing provision, educational equity — that a constitutional obligation would require to fulfill. You build the infrastructure before the constitutional requirement because the constitutional requirement, when it arrives, must be able to deliver. South Africa's Grootboom applicant died in a shack because the floor existed without the delivery infrastructure beneath it. The reconstruction builds the infrastructure first.

The constitutional track runs through three mechanisms in sequence. State constitutional amendments come first — requiring only a state legislative supermajority or citizen referendum, immediately enforceable in state courts, demonstrating that the abundance orientation is politically viable. Montana's 1972 children's rights language provides the model text. South Africa's Section 28 provides the substantive list. A state constitutional amendment establishing children's rights to basic nutrition, healthcare, shelter, education, and protection from exploitation is achievable in California, New York, Illinois, Washington, and Colorado in the near term.

Federal constitutional amendment comes second, building on the state-level demonstration. The Nineteenth Amendment required a century of sustained advocacy before the three-fourths threshold could be reached. The reconstruction follows the same sequencing: pilot at the state level, document the outcomes, build the coalition on demonstrated evidence, bring the federal amendment when the demonstration is complete. The Demeny voting proposal runs alongside both tracks — piloted at the state level, with the AI-assisted civic education and questionnaire providing the stewardship framework that simple proxy voting lacked. The proxy vote and the constitutional amendment address different structural problems: one addresses absent representation, the other addresses the absent floor. A child who is constitutionally represented in the political process and constitutionally entitled to the floors of her development is the child the Preamble announced and the provisions abandoned.

THE SPECIFIC LANGUAGE of the proposed amendment, drawn from South Africa's Section 28, the UN Convention on the Rights of the Child, Montana's children's rights provision, and Germany's Basic Law:

Every child has the right to the conditions necessary for healthy development, including basic nutrition, shelter, healthcare, education, and protection from exploitation, neglect, and abuse. The state shall take reasonable and progressive measures, within available resources, to realize these rights for all children within its jurisdiction. No child shall be deprived of these rights on the basis of the immigration status, income, race, or national origin of herself or her parents.

Every child shall be recognized as a legal subject with full standing in courts and political processes to enforce these rights.

Four provisions. The first establishes the affirmative floor — the specific list the child test has identified as the conditions of human development, drawn from the international frameworks that represent the accumulated consensus of the nations that have addressed this question seriously. The second establishes the implementation standard — reasonable and progressive measures within available resources — the South African standard, proven in litigation, honest about what states can immediately deliver while enforceable against states that make no effort. The third extends the floor to the children the existing constitutional architecture has defined out of posterity — immigrant children, children in detention, every child whose existence the document counts for apportionment but not for protection. The fourth establishes the legal standing that makes the floor justiciable — the child as original legal subject, not merely a recipient of parental rights. This language is not radical. Every provision is grounded in international frameworks that dozens of democracies have already adopted and enforced. The radical claim is not the language. The radical claim is that the United States — the country whose Preamble announced the obligation to posterity two and a half centuries ago — should finally align its constitutional architecture with its founding announcement.

THE RECONSTRUCTION IS NOT a single event. It is a generational commitment — the incremental democratic process that the Nordic societies used to build the abundance orientation into their constitutional cultures over a century, now available to a society that has seen the pattern clearly enough to pursue it deliberately. At every stage — each state amendment, each federal program, each

Demeny voting pilot, each AI-assisted constitutional audit — the question is the same one the founders wrote into the Preamble and never answered in the provisions: what does this produce for the child with no buffer between herself and what it delivers?

The answer the reconstruction is building toward is what Finland produces. What Norway produces. What Germany produces, increasingly. What Ambedkar tried to produce, and what the children of South Africa are still trying to hold their government to. What the children of Montana have just produced, from a constitutional provision dormant for fifty years until they applied it. It is a child who exists, and whose existence the foundational document of her society recognizes as the obligation it has always announced. Not because she has earned it. Not because her parents have the resources to purchase it. Because she exists. Because the Preamble said posterity. Because the word was always there. The reconstruction does not ask the document to become something it was not designed to be. It asks the document to become what it announced it was for.

O Humanity

– RNB

O humanity —
human, all too human.

You and the leaders you produce
were all children not too long ago.
And forever.

The feelings you carry —
the fear at the bottom,
the grief in the middle,
the reason at the top —
were laid down before you could speak.
They run through your leaders
as they run through you.

Crowds amplify.
Enemies multiply.
The frightened man
produces the frightened room
produces the frightened document

produces the frightened generation.

This is not destiny.
It is a bottom layer
that has not yet been seen.

See it.

Let the child be your guide.
Serve the child and posterity
and you need not fear anything
or anyone —
unified in a common goal
that no enemy can contest,
because it belongs to all of them too.

Their children are waiting
as yours are.

Epilogue: Posterity

The word is in the first sentence. We the People of the United States, in Order to form a more perfect Union, establish Justice, insure domestic Tranquility, provide for the common defence, promote the general Welfare, and secure the Blessings of Liberty to ourselves and our Posterity, do ordain and establish this Constitution for the United States of America. Posterity. The founders wrote it themselves. Not the people in the room. The ones who would come after — the children, the grandchildren, the generations who would inherit what the room produced without having been consulted about its design. The obligation to posterity is not an interpretation of the Preamble. It is the Preamble's announced purpose, stated in its first and only sentence, before a single provision follows. The provisions never caught up to the announcement.

This book began as a clinical observation: every policy failure the Abundance Series documented across five volumes had a deeper cause than policy. The healthcare system that fails children, the education system that underdelivers, the criminal justice system that criminalizes poverty, the housing policy that concentrates deprivation, the environmental degradation that children will spend their lives inheriting — all of these trace back to the same foundational layer. The constitutional architecture. The founding choice. The room in Philadelphia in the summer of 1787 where specific men, under specific pressures, made specific decisions that encoded the scarcity orientation into the document that would govern everything downstream.

The book performed a revaluation. Not a condemnation — the founders were real people who achieved something real under extraordinary pressure, and the mythology that surrounds their work serves genuine purposes. A revaluation in the Nietzschean sense: returning to the founding values and asking what they are for, who they serve, and whether the machinery built to honor them is delivering what the founding announcement said it was for. The child test was the instrument. Applied without ideology, without the mythological scaffolding that makes the design invisible, to the American Constitution and to the comparative constitutional evidence of what other founding moments produced, the child test finds a consistent pattern: the document does not deliver what its Preamble announced to the child who has no buffer between herself and what the provisions actually require. And other founding moments — driven by different traumas, encoding different orientations — produced different floors, different outcomes, different children. The founding choice was not inevitable. That is the book's central clinical finding. It was a choice made under specific conditions, by specific people, with specific limitations. Other conditions produced other choices. The design can be changed. The reconstruction is available.

~

The child has been present throughout this book. She appeared before Chapter One — the child who speaks from the body's wisdom, who has not learned blindness yet and claims that as her only credential. She appeared in the South African Constitution's

Section 28 and in Ambedkar's classroom floor and in the Finnish baby box and in the Norwegian oil fund and in the Ecuadorian Pachamama. She appeared in Joshua DeShaney's file, in the caseworker's prediction, in the majority opinion that required nothing. She appeared in the immigration detention facility and in the rubble of Gaza and Kharkiv. She appeared in the 3.7 million children who re-entered poverty in January 2022 when one senator blocked a renewal. She appeared in the Montana courtroom, five years old, arguing that the constitution her state wrote in 1972 meant what it said.

She is not a metaphor. She is the measure. Every constitutional provision, every policy choice, every institutional design — what does it produce for her? That is the question the founders wrote into the Preamble and the provisions have never fully answered. The answer this book has documented is honest and incomplete in exactly the right proportion. Honest: the American constitutional architecture as it stands does not provide the floor. The child at the bottom has no constitutional claim to the conditions of her development. The policy argument has been losing for decades not because the evidence is insufficient but because the argument is being made in the wrong register — as a plea for better policy inside an architecture designed to resist it. Incomplete: the founding choice was not inevitable, the reconstruction is available, the window is open, the evidence from Montana and Helsinki and Pretoria and Berlin shows what a different choice produces. The incompleteness is the hope.

The Abundance Series has argued across six books that the scarcity orientation and the abundance orientation are not equally matched forces. The scarcity orientation self-devours. The abundance orientation compounds. Over time — the timescale of constitutional democracy, of generational change, of the incremental accumulation of better choices — the abundance orientation wins. Not automatically. Not without the sustained advocacy, the clarity of diagnosis, the specific instruments this book has identified. But structurally, over the long arc. The self-devouring cycle consumes itself. The compounding cycle builds.

The child is the evidence. The Finnish child who received the baby box grows up to report the highest life satisfaction on earth. The Montana child who argued a constitutional provision into enforcement at the age of five is doing what the Preamble always invited: holding the document to its own announced purpose. The South African child who can invoke Section 28 in court has a claim the American child does not — and the existence of that claim, even when imperfectly fulfilled, is closer to what the founding announcement required than its absence. The child is also the instruction. Let the posterity and the child be your guide, the Author's Voice poem says, and you will not dehumanize. This is not sentiment. It is the clinical argument in its most concentrated form: the child's abundance orientation — the openness, the trust, the embodied knowing that preceded every learned defense — is the abundance orientation the founding documents encoded in their preambles and abandoned in their provisions. The revaluation returns to that orientation. The reconstruction builds from it.

~

The word posterity has been waiting in the Preamble for two hundred and thirty-eight years. It is still there. It has always been there. The founders wrote it, perhaps without fully understanding what they were committing to, perhaps knowing exactly what they were committing to and encoding it in the one place the provisions would never have to fulfill it. Either way, the word is there. The obligation it announces is there. The children who will inherit what is built in this generation are coming. They are always coming. Posterity is not a historical category. It is the permanent condition of a document designed to govern across time.

The reconstruction this book proposes is not a revolution. It is a completion. The Preamble announced the purpose. The provisions have been catching up to it for two and a half centuries — through abolition, through suffrage, through civil rights, through every amendment that extended the founding promise to the people the founding compact excluded. The completion asks only what every generation has eventually been asked: are you willing to build what the Preamble announced? Are you willing to write the floor that the child at the bottom requires, so that the blessings of liberty are not reserved for those lucky enough to be born above it?

The child test is simple. The child is waiting. The word is in the first sentence. It has always been there.

A Final Word

Mahatma Gandhi was on a hunger strike. Hindus and Muslims — neighbors who had known each other all their lives — were massacring one another across the subcontinent. The violence diminished as Gandhi weakened. Then it stopped. People could not watch him die.

An angry Hindu man approached him. He said: they killed my ten-year-old son. I want to kill one of their children. How do I deal with this feeling?

Gandhi said, calmly: Find a Muslim boy who is orphaned and alone. Adopt him. Raise him in his faith as your own.

That is the child test applied to the worst moment in human life. Not consolation. Not ideology. Not the request for patience. A child. Another child. The orphaned child as the path back from the abyss of grief. There was no room for rationalization. There never is when the answer is specific enough. Find that boy. Raise him as he is. The angry man had no place to put his anger when the answer was that concrete, that human, and that generous.

Every war. Every conflict. Every neighbor turned into an enemy. Every founding compact that excludes the people it should protect. Every constitutional document that announces posterity and abandons it in the provisions. The principle holds across all of them: the child is the guide. Not because the child is innocent or pure or free from the complexity of human life — but because the child is the common future. Your child and your enemy's child are waiting in the same gap. The document that serves one and not the other has not yet understood what it is for.

Gandhi understood. He was near death and he understood. The abundance orientation does not require strength or safety or prosperity to operate. It requires only the willingness to see another person's child and recognize your own.

The reconstruction this book proposes begins there. Not in Philadelphia. Not in a courtroom. In the moment when a grieving man is given an answer he cannot rationalize away.

Afterword

As I am rereading and listening to this book, I am inspired with more ideas. Feelings rule human decisions. Feelings are layered — with the deepest and most recent ones perhaps going back to early development during the attachment phase in infancy, itself colored by inherent temperament and the complex inheritance of caretakers. This is the bottom layer, resilient or more fixed but dynamic, interlaying with all the other layers as the floor. Feelings are very contagious, producing even more complexity. Groups — like crowds — enhance the group feelings and decisions even more, polarized this way or that. True friends and advisors provide a broader perspective, like my friends did in writing these books, helping see through the blind spots.

AI helped further with research, revising and rewriting in real time. What would have taken a year to write could be accomplished in weeks. As I have worked with AI over the last two years, AI has improved with leaps and bounds. As I go over this book, I realize that great leaders in different states of mind produced different founding documents, colored by their sentiments and fears. I realize that the child test and posterity as a guiding principle is of paramount importance for leaders — to get out of their own heads and think of the future as the collective future of humanity, which includes everyone, even foes.

Then a poem came to mind.

O humanity, human, all too human.
You and the leaders you produce were all children not too long ago, and forever.
Let the child be your guide.
Serve the child and posterity, then you need not fear anything or anyone, unified in a common goal.

This ended with an anecdote I remember from Mahatma Gandhi's life. He went on a hunger strike in response to Hindus and Muslims — neighbors — turned into enemies, massacring each other. Violence diminished and then came to a halt as Mahatma was nearing his own demise. An angry Hindu man approached him and said: they killed my ten-year-old son and now I want to kill one of the Muslim children. How do I deal with this feeling? Mahatma Gandhi said calmly: Find a Muslim boy who is orphaned and alone, and adopt him. Raise him in his faith as your own.

That is the piercing insight of a great man despite profound adversity and scarcity. It left no room for rationalization. Every war, every conflict — neighbor killing neighbor — could be reduced to insignificance and even eliminated with this principle in mind.

~

I am evolving. So can the reader. So can the leader. So can humanity. What this writing process has shown me is that the abundance orientation is not a fixed state you arrive at. It is a direction of travel. The book kept giving as I re-engaged with it. The ideas in it met my mind again, differently than before, and produced something neither the first writing nor the first reading could have reached alone. That is what the abundance orientation looks like in practice — not a destination, but a way of moving through the world that generates more than it consumes.

If this book has done that for one reader — if one leader has found, in the child test or in Gandhi's answer, something they could not rationalize away — then the work has found its purpose. The word posterity is still in the first sentence. You are still reading. That is enough to begin.

Ravinder Nath Bhalla, MD
Ridgewood, New Jersey · March 2026

Index

The Darker Scenario

A FURTHER WORD ON WHY THE RECONSTRUCTION CANNOT WAIT

Patrick Henry did not sign the Constitution. He refused to attend the Philadelphia Convention — he said he smelled a rat. When Virginia's ratifying convention debated the document in 1788, he delivered some of the most prescient speeches in American political history. He warned that the general welfare clause and the necessary and proper clause would eventually concentrate power in a federal government accountable to no one the ordinary citizen could reach. He warned that the executive the document created could become, in practice, a king. He warned that the document's protections were procedural shells that a determined political actor could learn to wear while hollowing them out. He was not arguing against the Constitution because he preferred anarchy. He was arguing for a document with a genuine floor — one whose protections extended to the people who would actually need them, not only to the people with the standing to invoke them.

The Brutus essays, published in New York during the ratification debates, made the same argument with greater legal precision. Brutus No. 1 argued that the Constitution's grant of power was effectively unlimited — that the supremacy clause, the necessary and proper clause, and the general welfare language together gave the federal government authority to do whatever it judged necessary, regardless of what the states or the people thought. The Anti-Federalists lost that debate. The Constitution was ratified. And Brutus's prediction has been, across two and a half centuries, substantially correct. What neither Henry nor Brutus fully articulated — because they could not yet see it — was the mechanism by which the absent floor would eventually threaten the walls they were trying to protect.

Friedrich Nietzsche, writing a century after the founding, described the conditions under which what he called the great man of the masses emerges. He was not celebrating this figure. He was diagnosing a mechanism. In periods of nihilism — when the old values have collapsed and no new ones have been established — in periods of decadence and despair and polarization, a vacuum of meaning opens. Into that vacuum comes the figure who channels resentment rather than reason. Who names the enemy as the explanation for the suffering the absent floor has produced. Who offers the scarcity orientation in its most concentrated and most dangerous form: I will give you what the constitutional order has denied you, and in exchange you will give me the power to dismantle the order that denied it. This is the authoritarian bargain. It has a logic that despair makes compelling.

The absent floor does not only harm the child. It produces, across generations, the political conditions that make the authoritarian bargain legible. A population living without the floor — without the basic conditions of human development, without economic security, without trust that the institutions are for them — is a population susceptible to the leader who promises to tear down the walls on their behalf. The walls the founders built to protect liberty become, in the hands of a polarized population living without the floor, the obstacle between the people and what they have been told they deserve. This is the mechanism the Anti-Federalists feared without being able to fully name. The walls alone cannot protect a republic whose floor has been absent long enough to produce the despair that makes the walls negotiable.

The present moment is not named here because this book is not a political document about any specific leader or party. It does not need to be. The mechanism operates independent of the specific figures it produces. What can be observed clinically, without partisan framing, is this: the conditions Nietzsche described as preconditions for authoritarian capture — nihilism, despair, polarization, decadence, institutional distrust — are the predictable downstream products of a constitutional architecture that has maintained an absent floor for two and a half centuries. The deaths of despair documented by Case and Deaton. The child poverty rate that is the highest of any wealthy democracy. The gerrymandering and voting restrictions that have followed the collapse of preclearance protections against voting discrimination. The twenty-eight states that have filed Article V convention applications — applications driven primarily not by the goal of building a floor but by the goal of removing walls.

The reconstruction this book proposes is not idealistic. It is the only structural alternative to the authoritarian bargain. Build the floor through democratic process — incrementally, at the state level first, through the sustained advocacy that eventually produced women's suffrage and civil rights — or watch the floor be promised by the authoritarian at the price of the walls. There is no third path. A population in sufficient despair, without sufficient floor, will eventually accept the bargain. History has confirmed this more than once. The founders feared it. The Anti-Federalists named it. Nietzsche described the mechanism. The present moment is demonstrating it.

The child test applied to this scenario finds the same result it always finds: the child at the bottom, the child who has no buffer between herself and what the constitutional architecture actually delivers, is the person most harmed when the floor is absent and the first person sacrificed when the authoritarian bargain is struck. She was not consulted about the founding compact. She was not consulted about the bargain. She inherits both.

The reconstruction is not optional. It is the answer to the only question that matters:

what do you build before the bargain becomes irresistible?

Build the floor. Before it is too late to choose.

Ravinder Nath Bhalla, MD
Ridgewood, New Jersey · March 2026

A Note on Sources

This book draws on primary sources, legal cases, historical scholarship, and clinical literature. What follows is not a complete bibliography but a guide to the most important sources for each part of the argument, offered so that readers who want to go further have a clear path.

THE FOUNDING MOMENT

The primary record of the Constitutional Convention is James Madison's Notes of Debates in the Federal Convention of 1787, available in multiple editions and online through the Avalon Project at Yale Law School. Madison's notes are the closest thing we have to a daily account of the convention's deliberations — not a verbatim transcript, but a remarkably full record of the arguments made and the choices taken. Robert Yates's notes, published as Secret Proceedings and Debates of the Convention, offer a useful counterpoint. For the ratification debates, The Federalist Papers — numbers 10, 41, 49, and 51 are most relevant to this book's argument — and the Anti-Federalist responses collected in The Anti-Federalist Papers and the Constitutional Convention Debates, edited by Ralph Ketcham, are essential.

On the Declaration of Independence and the deleted slave trade clause, Pauline Maier's American Scripture: Making the Declaration of Independence provides the most thorough account of the drafting process. On the founders' psychology and the convention's dynamics, Michael Klarman's The Framers' Coup: The Making of the United States Constitution is the most recent and most comprehensive scholarly treatment.

THE CONSTITUTIONAL CASES

DeShaney v. Winnebago County of Social Services, 489 U.S. 189 (1989), is available in full through the Supreme Court's website and through legal databases. Both Rehnquist's majority opinion and Brennan's dissent repay careful reading in their entirety. Shelby County v. Holder, 570 U.S. 529 (2013), and Rucho v. Common Cause, 588 U.S. 684 (2019), are similarly available. For a comprehensive analysis of what the Constitution does and does not require the state to provide, Cass Sunstein and Stephen Holmes's The Cost of Rights: Why Liberty Depends on Taxes remains the clearest argument that all rights, including negative rights, require affirmative state action to be meaningful.

COMPARATIVE CONSTITUTIONAL LAW

The South African Constitution of 1996, the German Basic Law of 1949, and the Nordic constitutions are all available in English translation online. For comparative analysis, Ran Hirschl's Comparative Matters: The Renaissance of Comparative Constitutional Law and Mark Tushnet's Weak Courts, Strong Rights: Judicial Review and Social Welfare Rights in Comparative Constitutional Law are the most relevant scholarly treatments. On B.R. Ambedkar and the Indian Constitution, Gail Omvedt's Ambedkar: Towards an Enlightened India provides accessible background.

DEATHS OF DESPAIR

Anne Case and Angus Deaton's Deaths of Despair and the Future of Capitalism (2020) is the primary source for the mortality data discussed in Chapter Four. Deaton's earlier work, The Great Escape: Health, Wealth, and the Origins of Inequality, provides essential context. For the connection between constitutional design and social outcomes, comparative data is available through the OECD, the World Health Organization, and the United Nations Human Development Index.

THE ABUNDANCE SERIES

The five preceding volumes in this series — Abundance: Beyond Scarcity and Self-Devouring Cycles; The Two Minds: Choosing Abundance over Scarcity; Red Lines Rising: Governing AI While We Still Can; The Abundance Dispatch: Letters to Power; and Building Abundance: What We Ought to Create — develop the framework applied in this book to the constitutional layer. Readers who want the full clinical and philosophical foundation for the scarcity and abundance orientations will find it there.

THE CLINICAL FRAMEWORK

The identification with the aggressor concept originates with Sándor Ferenczi and was developed by Anna Freud in The Ego and the Mechanisms of Defense (1936). For its application to group psychology and institutional behavior, the most relevant work is Judith Herman's Trauma and Recovery. On the developmental psychology underlying the child test, the foundational texts are John Bowlby's Attachment and Loss trilogy and Daniel Siegel's The Developing Mind. Friedrich Nietzsche's concept of revaluation, central to Part Three, is developed most accessibly in Thus Spoke Zarathustra and On the Genealogy of Morality.

Acknowledgments

This book is the product of forty years of clinical work, five previous volumes, and the conversations — in clinics, in classrooms, in policy rooms, and in the quiet of the writing — that shaped every argument in it. The children and families I have worked with across four decades of practice are the real authors of the child test. They taught it to me before I had words for it.

The Abundance Series has been sustained by readers, colleagues, and thinkers who engaged seriously with its arguments across six books. Their challenges strengthened every chapter. Particular gratitude is owed to the legal scholars, constitutional historians, comparative law researchers, and child welfare advocates whose published work underlies the research this book draws on. The Cowork AI research platform contributed the systematic constitutional and legal research that grounds Part Two and Part Three — a live demonstration of the civic reasoning function that Chapter Eleven argues AI can serve.

The errors that remain are mine alone.

Further Reading

Primary Constitutional Documents

Madison, James. Notes of Debates in the Federal Convention of 1787 (avalon.law.yale.edu). The Federalist Papers, Numbers 10, 41, 49, and 51. The Anti-Federalist Papers, including Brutus No. 1 and the Letters of the Federal Farmer (oll.libertyfund.org). Constitution of South Africa, 1996 — especially Sections 10, 26, 27, 28, and 29. Constitution of the Federal Republic of Germany (Basic Law), 1949 — especially Articles 1 and 20. Constitution of Finland, 2000 — especially Section 19. Constitution of Norway — especially Article 112. UN Convention on the Rights of the Child, 1989 (unicef.org).

Key Case Law

DeShaney v. Winnebago County, 489 U.S. 189 (1989). Town of Castle Rock v. Gonzales, 545 U.S. 748 (2005). San Antonio Independent School District v. Rodriguez, 411 U.S. 1 (1973). Plyler v. Doe, 457 U.S. 202 (1982). Helvering v. Davis, 301 U.S. 619 (1937). NFIB v. Sebelius, 567 U.S. 519 (2012). Rucho v. Common Cause, 588 U.S. 684 (2019). Shelby County v. Holder, 570 U.S. 529 (2013). Government of South Africa v. Grootboom, 2000 (4) SA 1 (CC). Minister of Health v. Treatment Action Campaign, 2002 (5) SA 721

(CC). German Federal Constitutional Court, Hartz IV Decision, 1 BvL 1/09 (2010). Held v. State of Montana, Montana Supreme Court (2024).

Recommended Books

Sunstein, Cass R., and Stephen Holmes. The Cost of Rights: Why Liberty Depends on Taxes. Norton, 1999. — Sabato, Larry. A More Perfect Constitution. Walker and Company, 2007. — Hirschl, Ran. Comparative Matters: The Renaissance of Comparative Constitutional Law. Oxford University Press, 2014. — Ambedkar, B.R. Annihilation of Caste. Multiple editions. — Case, Anne, and Angus Deaton. Deaths of Despair and the Future of Capitalism. Princeton University Press, 2020. — Kleinfeld, Joshua, and Stephen Sachs. Give Parents the Vote. Notre Dame Law Review 100:3 (2024). — Klarman, Michael. The Framers' Coup: The Making of the United States Constitution. Oxford University Press, 2016.

Data Sources

UNICEF Innocenti Report Card 19: Child Wellbeing in Rich Countries (2025). — World Happiness Report 2025. UN Sustainable Development Solutions Network. — Columbia University Center on Poverty and Social Policy: Monthly Child Poverty Reports (2021–2022). — OECD Family Database: Child Wellbeing Indicators. — McKinsey Global Institute: The Economic Potential of Generative AI (2023). — Magesh et al. Hallucination-Free? Assessing the Reliability of Leading AI Legal Research Tools. Journal of Empirical Legal Studies (2025).

Also by the Author

The Abundance Series

Book One *Abundance: Beyond Scarcity and Self-Devouring Cycles*

Book Two *The Two Minds: Choosing Abundance over Scarcity*

Book Three *Red Lines Rising: Governing AI While We Still Can*

Book Four *The Abundance Dispatch: Letters to Power*

Book Five *Building Abundance: What We Ought to Create*

About the Author

Ravinder Nath Bhalla, MD is a child and adolescent psychiatrist with forty years of clinical practice, primarily with children and families in underserved communities across the United States. He immigrated to the United States from India in 1982. His clinical work has focused on the intersection of child development, mental health, and the institutional systems — child welfare, education, criminal justice — that shape what children receive and what they are denied. He is the author of the six-volume Abundance Series, which applies a clinical framework distinguishing the scarcity orientation from the abundance orientation across the full range of human organization, from the individual mind to the founding document. He is nearly sixty-eight years old, eighty percent retired, and lives in New Jersey.

Made in the USA
Monee, IL
13 September 2026

62976629R00095